# Methodology and Meanings

## Viewpoints in Sociology

# Methodology and Meanings

## Varieties of Sociological Inquiry

George V. Zito

PRAEGER PUBLISHERS

New York • Washington

Published in the United States of America in 1975
by Praeger Publishers, Inc.
111 Fourth Avenue, New York, N.Y. 10003

© 1975 by Praeger Publishers, Inc.

Library of Congress Cataloging in Publication Data

Zito, George V
  Methodology and meanings.

  Bibliography: p.
  1. Sociology—Methodology. 2. Sociological research. 3. Social change.
I. Title.
HM24.Z54          301'.01'8          74-10649
ISBN 0-275-51110-3

Printed in the United States of America

# Contents

# Editor's Foreword

## by Arthur Vidich

THE VIEWPOINTS IN SOCIOLOGY SERIES seeks to transmit to the beginning student a sense of the sociological attitude, of how he can use sociology to learn about his world. *Methodology and Meanings* introduces procedures for collecting and interpreting data from the viewpoint that they are means to the broader end of comprehending our lives.

In the past several decades, sociology has seen the development of new methodologies and more refined techniques of research. It has incorporated and absorbed modern computer technologies and complex methods of statistical analysis. Sociologists have become much more aware of how they do their work; this is reflected in the notable increase in articles and books devoted solely to questions of methods and methodologies.

When a field of science becomes too self-conscious about its methods of investigation, this is usually a sign that its attention has been deflected from its primary concern: knowledge of the real world. A method is, after all, simply a procedure we use to arrive at a solution to a problem. In this sense, the methods and tools used by a carpenter to build a house have the same status as the methods and tools used by a sociologist to discover something about the social world. The carpenter who cannot cut a board until he has sharpened his saw to a state of perfection cannot take the first step in constructing a house. Similarly, sociologists have at times not studied problems because they have felt their methods to be insufficient to the task. The first sentences of many monographs have not been written because the pencil was never sharp enough. A science, just like a craft, begins with problems and out of necessity develops its methods.

It is a major virtue of Professor George Zito's work that he has not separated his discussion of methods from the problems of the world. He aptly notes, "The world is constantly changing in ways that we never imagined it could or would," and he treats methods—as is indicated in his subtitle, *Varieties of Sociological Inquiry*—as varying procedures that we use to discover relevant facts and possible solutions to the problems we pose for ourselves.

*Methodology and Meanings* introduces the student to the full spectrum of the tools of sociological research. Quantitative and qualitative methods are treated separately and in relation to each other. The basic forms of statistical analysis and the fundamental paradigms of research design are presented in the context of real, meaningful problems confronted by the practicing sociologist. Research procedures such as content analysis, surveys, and participant observation, which are the stock in trade of the sociological enterprise, are discussed in separate chapters. In another chapter, Professor Zito shows a special concern for historiographic research and for the interplay between theory and research. I know of no other book that presents research methods in so concise and directly comprehensible a manner. I am pleased to welcome this study to the Viewpoints in Sociology series.

# Preface and Acknowledgments

PROBABLY NO PHENOMENON is of greater interest to the student than social change. Not only do we live in the midst of social change; we are ourselves constantly changing, and it is not always clear that the changes within us are synchronized with the changes we see about us. "What's happening?" is no mere rhetorical question. Very often we feel that we have somehow been left out, that we cannot catch up, that the world is changing in ways we never imagined it could or would.

The poet A. E. Housman wrote,

> I, a stranger and afraid
> In a world I never made,

and thus gave expression to the growing sense of alienation experienced by the individual in modern society. But as Louis Schneider, an American sociologist, has recently noted, men do indeed make the world they inhabit, although to a large extent they do so inadvertently. And just as the road to Hell is paved with good intentions, so, too, the results of our intentions are often less gratifying than those that we anticipated.

The age-old dream of being able to "dominate history," to make the world into the kind of place we know it has the capacity to become, seems today as elusive as ever. In America, for example, something appears to have died with the student strikes of 1970. Institutionalized society—an abstraction existing primarily in the minds of men—somehow frustrated our best efforts to introduce major change. How can such a thing happen? How can relationships between individuals and organizations be so structured that they not only resist but outlast the people who participate in them? How is society possible? Every major social theorist has struggled with this question. There is, to this day, no definitive answer; we do not know.

But we do know that society is not static; it is dynamic, constantly changing, although not always in the direction of our "best intentions." We both make society and are made by it; there is continual interaction between ourselves as individuals and the collective reality in which we find ourselves. Those whom C. Wright Mills referred to as "armchair sociologists" are content to sit on the sidelines, reflecting on the mad human comedy and offering comments on it from their distant perspective. Other sociologists are directly involved in the activity surrounding them and seek only to describe it accurately. Still others perform controlled experiments or make measurements with which they hope to gauge those elements that persist and those that change. There are as many varieties of sociology as there are sociologists.

I confess that I am so dissatisfied with each method of sociological investigation that I am forced to be completely eclectic, using a bit of this one and more of that one, hoping that if I employ a sufficient number of different approaches to analyze the phenomenon, I might be able to catch a glimpse of some underlying fact or truth and extract something of meaning. I find social reality too complex to yield to any single quantitative or qualitative method, however sophisticated. Trapped in a reality constantly undergoing change while I myself undergo change, I never feel methodologically secure. All my conclusions are tentative; I reserve the right to try again and come up with a different explanation the next time around. And it is this attitude that I seek to inculcate in the sudent. Any judgment that we, as sociologists, may make is wholly tentative and subject to change. To be scientific we must reserve the right to change our minds in the face of new evidence.

This does not mean that we have the right to be irresponsible or downright sloppy in our investigations—quite the contrary. It means that we must be as systematic and as precise as we possibly can be. It means that we must muster all the resources we have at our disposal and make a concerted assault on the problem at hand. I know of no other way of learning to do this than by attempting to understand the available research methodologies. This involves applying them to representative samples and getting the "feel" of how they work and why they work the way they do. It means learning enough about them so that we know both their strengths and their weaknesses. Research methods are the tools of social science, and there is no possible way of working at any endeavor without employing appropriate tools. If we are aware that our tools have limitations, and if we *know* these limitations, we can make appropriate allowances in our results. Only if we do make such allowances can our results have any substantive meaning. And it is *meaning* that lies at the center of all our sociological efforts.

## How the Text Is Organized

Since I feel that a student can learn research methodology only by doing it, I have arranged the text in a manner that involves him immediately. Part I is an introduction to some basic concepts and to the analytical method generally. Part II covers content analysis, survey research, and participant observation, in that order. In employing content analysis the student works by himself, using readily obtainable documents, books, and written communications. Since his (or her) research materials are fixed, the student may go back to the sample repeatedly and recheck the data derived from it. In survey research we are required to work with others, whom we interview; here we are less secure, since the sample, once transformed into coded data, is no longer available to us at the time of our analysis. In participant observation we must not only work with others but do so in a highly controlled manner, further compounding the methodological problem. Thus, the text is arranged progressively. While one is learning these techniques, one is also building upon them and learning additional basic concepts applicable to research generally. At the conclusion of these chapters, I have included representative samples of undergraduate research that can serve as models for the student's own efforts.

Part III introduces some of the problems associated with conceptualization. It stresses precision and takes a "harder" look at some of the concepts considered in earlier chapters, placing them within a more rigorous frame of reference. This section also considers some recent methodological techniques and prepares the student for more advanced course work. Most important, it encourages a critical attitude in examining the reported work of others and in improving one's own techniques.

This book is intended as a first course in research methodology. Its aim is to teach research at the level of meanings and to demonstrate that all social research employs analytical method. A previous course in statistics is not required; indeed, some will see this text as providing a new de-emphasis on quantitative methods. The basic concepts used here are applicable to the analytical process generally, whether or not statistical measures are employed to supplement them. The goal of social research is, after all, an understanding of social reality, not the institutionalization of some particular research methodology.

I would like to acknowledge the many helpful criticisms received from colleagues and students in the preparation of this text. Portions of the manuscript were read by Jerry Jacobs, Howard Taylor, Ephraim Mizruchi, and Stanford Lyman. The index was prepared by Karina O'Malley and Ellen Adams. It was Arthur Vidich who suggested my doing the book and offered many helpful suggestions. Gladys Topkis of Praeger was the most helpful editor one could wish for. The book is dedicated to my wife, Dorothea, who assisted in its preparation in more ways than I can possibly enumerate or thank her for.

# I
# Introduction

# 1

# *Theory* vs. *Methodology*

THE SEARCH FOR MEANING is older than the scientific method. Herodotus, the Greek historian who lived in the fifth century B.C., tells us that in the earliest days of Greece the teleologists explained all phenomena with the formula "Zeus first, Zeus last, all things Zeus," thus attributing a divine purpose to every aspect of reality. The teleologists, Herodotus says, were replaced by the *physikoi*, who sought explanations by looking for the antecedent causes of events. As one might suspect, the conflict between teleology and physics (or science) was never completely settled, although science appears to have made the greater advances since the time of Descartes (1590–1605) and Newton (1642–1727). While most sociologists, particularly those who call themselves "social scientists," consider teleological explanations unacceptable, this primitivism occasionally manages to intrude itself into otherwise scientific discussion.

This is especially true today. In the desperate search for community in which human values will be preserved, some people advocate the abandonment of rigorous method and procedures, in the hope that some universal *OM* will provide a solution to problems that are, to say the least, distinctly human. Most of us, however, as heirs of the humanistic tradition, insist that if humanity's problem is to be solved—if, indeed, it is solvable—it will

3

be solved only by men and women applying that intelligence they have made use of in the past. No god will descend to set the world straight. We are the heirs of six thousand years of human thought. The words inscribed on the tombs of Egyptian kings prior to the invention of the pyramid express the same hopes and aspirations we find expressed today. "Man," Carl Sandburg wrote, "is a long time coming; Man will yet win."

Although not all of us may be capable of such faith, it is quite evident that, at other times than our own, societies found themselves confronted with what appeared to be insoluble social problems. This was particularly true of Periclean Athens and Elizabethan England and is reflected in the dramas of Euripides and Shakespeare. At periods of great social change, the world always appears to be in a state of ultimate collapse, and frantic calls are made for extrahuman solutions to the mess that humans alone have created.

Sociology, in league with the other social sciences, seeks a wholly human understanding of the complexity of social existence. Thus it aligns itself with the great humanistic tradition that, prior to Karl Marx (1818–83), was primarily the concern of literature, history, philosophy, science, and art. Although there had been excursions into social analysis as early as the Greeks, the application of scientific method in analyses of social phenomena is no older than the last century. Max Weber's sociological efforts were a reaction against Marx; Marx's thought also influenced Emile Durkheim and Georg Simmel. These four theorists dominate subsequent developments in sociology. Much, if not most, of what one reads in social science journals is an attempt to evaluate some aspect of their social theories.

This may come as a surprise to readers. Isn't sociology concerned with the social world *as it is,* rather than as some thinkers of the last century claimed it to be? Yes, of course. Anyone sufficiently learned to offer other explanations of society than those offered by Marx, Weber, Durkheim, and Simmel is, of course, quite free to do so. Occasional attempts are made. But such attempts usually turn out to be easily refuted by the most elementary methodological procedures. Marx, Weber, Durkheim, and Simmel (I list them in the order of their influence on subsequent thought) have survived not because teachers, professors, and book publishers are engaged in some kind of conspiracy to

promote them, but because they provide the greatest insights into
the social problem and are supported by the greatest body of
sociological research. We encourage graduate students in sociology to devise tests and conduct research aimed at refuting these
"giants." All sociologists would undoubtedly have a much easier
time of it if they could ignore these four and invent their own
"grand theories" (particularly since the work of these four contains points of contention, one with the others). But at least at
this stage of development, the "giants" will not surrender. About
thirty years ago, the prominent American sociologist Robert K.
Merton urged us to forget grand theory for a while and concen-
trate instead on "theories of the middle range," and this is the
course American sociology has largely taken. Although some
sociologists stop short of even middle-range theory and concen-
trate on description of kinds of events, the dominant emphasis
since Merton has been on attempts to relate such kinds of events
to a larger framework of theory short of a global approach.

Here, too, the reader is likely to express some surprise. How
important is theory? What does theory have to do with the social
reality we find about us? It should be pointed out at once that
method and theory cannot be divorced from each other: they
are two parts of the same thing. What we constantly seek is
*meaning*. We conduct an investigation in order to unearth this
meaning, but what we unearth can have no significance for us
unless we have some *frame of reference* in which it can be evaluated. An individual word has no meaning without other words
with which it can be employed and compared, and these are
bound together by certain theoretical rules of grammar and syntax. It makes little sense to weigh an object unless we have a
scale by means of which the object's weight may be compared
with the weights of other objects. In addition, we must be able
to relate *weight* to other properties, such as size and mass, for it
to have real meaning. Although this is transparently clear to the
student of physical and biological science, it escapes many beginning students of social science. "After all," he or she is apt to
feel, "I've been living in society all my life." This is almost
equivalent to asserting that one is an expert on biophysics because one has been a biological and physical entity all one's life.

If we are to find meaning in sociological inquiry, we must be
prepared to face a great deal of uncertainty and to challenge our

most precious prejudices and beliefs. Although it is relatively easy to challenge the attitudes, opinions, and life-styles of others, it is extremely difficult to attain the objectivity required to challenge one's own. We are each of us very certain that we see through the pretensions and bad taste of others, their glib allegiance to false gods and power drives. Each of us knows that he is not like other people, and each of us has gathered about him his own coterie of friends to provide the ideological reinforcement, the emotive support and personal reassurances necessary for him to go on doing what he "knows" is his own thing. That this *thing* has only been borrowed from a great many others at other times and other places is too confusing a prospect for us to face, unless we are dedicated to the search for meaning. "The unexamined life," Socrates declared, "is not worth living." One must appreciate the full weight of this statement and employ it as a methodological principle in one's social research. One must constantly re-examine one's own motives, one's own biases, one's own intentions in coming to any conclusions as a result of observations. We are always prone to see, in our results, only what we choose to see. We are always eager to tear down what is most precious to others without offering workable alternatives. A sociology that is *merely* iconoclastic does not explain or seek meaning. What is demanded of sociology by the times we live in is constructive insight upon which future possibilities may be shaped.

In writing the foregoing I have given expression to my own biases. The reader should take these biases into account in perusing the text that follows. This procedure, too, is a sound methodological principle, observed by many sociologists. It is the first principle I choose to impress upon the student.

## SOME ELEMENTARY CONCEPTS

Before undertaking research of any kind, it is important to have a definite methodology in mind and a well-planned research design. But even prior to this stage one must understand certain basic rules of analysis. Some of these rules will be discussed in connection with specific methodologies in the following chapters. There are, however, certain principles of analysis that are applicable, not only to sociological study but to studies of many other kinds. For example, a good English student, a good philosophy student, and a good geology student all know that the process of analysis requires constant comparison of two or more samples along fairly well-developed principles. We look for *similarities* and *differences* between the samples.

Thus, if we were comparing Shakespeare with Ben Jonson, we would note certain similarities: both men lived at the same time and in the same place, both wrote plays, both wrote poems, and so on—they are similar in many respects. But Shakespeare wrote more plays than Jonson, Jonson wrote about Shakespeare but Shakespeare did not write about Jonson, and so forth. Thus there are *differences*. This procedure, looking for what is the same and what is different, constitutes the comparative method. Whether we are comparing germs, atoms, chemical compounds, or cathedrals, comparison involves similarities and differences. Comparison is the basis of analysis. In evaluating the results of a sociological investigation, we must rely upon the same procedures as in any analysis.

Rather than pursuing the Shakespeare-Jonson analogy, I would like to generalize even further by employing a more abstract example. That is, I would like to move to a *higher level of abstraction*, one less specific than the previous one. What we discover here will, I hope, be applicable to a wider range of phenomena simply because it *is* more abstract.

Consider the two geometric figures shown in Figure 1–1. If we were forced to compare these two, what similarities and differences could we find?

Both figures appear to be squares, and they appear to be about the same size. They are, however, located differently on the page. But how can we determine whether in fact they *are* squares? *Theory* tells us that squares have equal sides and 90-degree internal angles. On this basis we might hypothesize that these two figures are squares, located differently on the page. We could then take a ruler and a protractor and measure the length of a side of A and then measure the other sides; we can do the same with B. Then, using the protractor, we could determine whether each angle is 90 degrees. We then could compare the dimensions and angles of A with those of B, looking for similarities

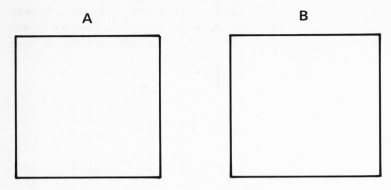

**Figure 1-1**

and differences. If all sides are equal and all angles are equal, we might want to assert that we have proved our hypothesis that both A and B are squares. But have we?

The scale we employed in measurement has discrete intervals marked upon it, fractions of inches. Unless our side length falls exactly upon such a mark, we cannot really know the exact line length. Our measurement could be a little off on any of the sides, in which case the figure would not be truly square. Perhaps B is closer to being a "true" square than A. Perhaps our protractor has insufficient accuracy to make us able to affirm that these angles are truly 90 degrees each. Thus there are possible sources of error in our measurements: one source is the accuracy of our instruments, the other the accuracy with which we employ the instruments. Because of such considerations, it would be precarious for us to assert that we have "proved" our hypothesis that these figures are squares. The most we can say is that *we cannot reject the hypothesis* that these figures are squares *on the basis of the instruments we have used in our measurements.* These instruments disclose A to be very similar to B in size and shape. About the only difference our instruments can disclose is that B lies closer to the right-hand margin of the paper than A, and that the two do not overlap each other and therefore are not one and the same figure but two separate figures. They are *probably* both squares.

In sociological research we very often compare two sets of numbers, two populations, two groups, two organizations, and the like. We employ scales other than inch scales, but our measurements are never more trustworthy than our scales (or instruments) and our accuracy in using them. The most we can ever do is fail to reject a hypothesis we have made. We can never *prove* a hypothesis true; we can only show, by means of analysis, that we are *able to reject it* or that we must *fail to reject it*. Failing to reject an assertion is not equivalent to *proving* it or to *accepting* the hypothesis. We are unable to control for all the possibilities involved in the geometry of A and B, for example. There are still possibilities that A and B are something other than squares. But on the basis of our measurements we cannot reject the probability that they are indeed squares. The *degree of confidence* we have in their being squares is, of course, a function of the accuracy of our measuring instruments and of our procedures in determining whether the figures meet the demands of the definition.

While emphasis on such simple notions may seem unnecessary, the student can be assured that, despite what has been said, he will find himself frequently making the error of asserting that he has "proved" his hypothesis, particularly in his early work. The point is so obvious that it appears to be trivial, but it is not; otherwise fine work is often marred by the researcher's neglect of the obvious.

Let us extend the example by considering Figure 1–2. Using the same instruments as previously, we fail to reject the hypothesis that these figures are squares. In the case of Figure 1–2, however, we feel a little uncomfortable. Luckily, we did not hypothesize that there were no differences (aside from location on the page)

Figure 1-2

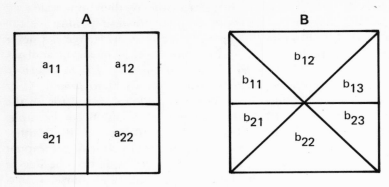

Figure 1-3

between A and B. If we had made such a hypothesis in regard to A and B of Figure 1–1, we would have been unable to reject it on the basis of our measurements. But how about Figure 1–2? Are we still unable to reject the hypothesis that there are no differences between A and B aside from location on the page? *On the basis of the instruments we have used,* we cannot reject the hypothesis, although our eyes perceive an obvious difference in the shading of Figure 1–2B. If we had included some instrument capable of measuring differences in shading, we would have rejected the hypothesis of no difference between A and B. This would have involved our employing three different scales or instruments, one for length, one for angle, and one for shading. We could have done this but neglected to see the possibility when we decided on instruments with which to compare A and B. Using protractor and scale, we can measure along only two dimensions, angularity and length. An instrument for measuring shading would have enabled us to measure a third dimension.

Now we must take a giant step to Figure 1–3. What are the similarities and differences between A and B of Figure 1–3? By the procedures previously employed, we would be unable to reject the hypothesis that both A and B are squares. Similarly, we would be unable to reject the hypothesis that they are the same size. But, employing our two limited instruments, we would have no trouble rejecting the hypothesis that there are no differences between A and B. There definitely *are* differences. Our measurements show that A has four components, each of which appears to be a square, while B has six components, and we reject the hypothesis that these components are squares. For the sake of identification, each component has been given a designation: a small letter matching the capital letter identifying the figure, and a subscript of two numbers showing the component's location in the figure. The first of these numbers shows the row in which the component is located, the second the column. Thus, in Figure 1–3, $a_{12}$ is in A and is located in the first row and the second column; $b_{23}$ is located in the second row and the third column of B. This kind of *matrix notation* is convenient when dealing with quantities arranged in rows and columns.

Upon examining A and B of Figure 1–3, it is apparent that there is more variation within B than within A. B has six components of equal size. A is *more homogeneous* than B, for it contains less variation. But there is little, if any, variation between A and B: Both appear to be squares of about equal size. Following our first analogy, this is similar to saying that there is more variation within Shakespeare's work than within Jonson's work. Yet both sets of work are from the same period, both have been composed by men, both consist of poetry, plays, and so on. Although they are similar sets of work, there is less variation *between* these sets than there is *within* them.

Comparing variations within and between groups of data is a procedure often employed in the analysis of sociological data. We shall have more to say about this in a later chapter, but for the moment it is worth noting that this is only one variant of the comparison method in analysis.

Figure 1–3 also helps to illustrate certain *logical fallacies* that researchers are very prone to commit. Consider B in Figure 1–3. It is a square composed of six members. It may also be considered a group of six parts, that is, a *group* of six *members*. Now, no one with any common sense would argue that since B has the property of squareness, all of its members must also possess the property of squareness. Obviously they are not square. Attributing to the members of a group the properties of that group is called the *ecological fallacy*. It is a fallacy to claim that since B is square, $b_{11}$, $b_{12}$, $b_{13}$, . . . $b_{23}$ must each also be square. This seems obvious in the present instance, but one may forget this when considering, for example, ghetto populations (i.e., groups) and the individual members living within the ghetto. It was

*Introduction*

indeed just such a misuse of sociological methods that led sociologist W. S. Robinson, as early as 1950, to consider its false
logic. Similarly, attributing to a group the properties of its
members is also a fallacy. We may not assert that, since $b_{23}$ is a
triangle, B must be a triangle. This is sometimes called the
*atomistic fallacy* but is more generally cited as an example of
what is termed *reductionism*. Reductionism involves attempting
to explain a collective phenomenon on the basis of individual
phenomena. In sociology, it is often charged that any attempt
to explain collective, or group, phenomena (sociological phenomena) on the basis of the psychology of individuals is reductionism and hence logically false. B is a whole, and its
properties may not be explained on the basis of the properties
of $b_{21}$ or $b_{22}$ or even $b_{11}$, . . . $b_{23}$. *The group must never be
confused with the individuals composing it.* A new group may be
composed of old members, and young persons may be members
of an old group; the Boy Scouts of America is older than any
person in it, and the recently formed Senior Citizens' groups are
younger than their old members.

There are many examples of logical fallacies. Reductionism
and the ecological fallacy are frequently encountered in sociological research; the first appears primarily in qualitative analysis
of data; the second appears most frequently in quantitative
analysis.

## QUANTITATIVE *vs.* QUALITATIVE

The reason these fallacies occur is easy to understand. Quantitative analysis recognizes that the laws governing large numbers
tend to make individual differences disappear and collective differences more apparent. Misuse of this principle can lead to
error. The Constitution of the United States, for example, requires that a census be taken at ten-year intervals, and such a
census contains a great deal of numerical information regarding
areas of the country. Some areas have high average annual in-
comes, while others, such as Appalachia, do not. Now, an *average*
income has nothing to do with an *individual* income. If in one
area we have ten people, each with an annual income of $12,000,
then the average income of that area is $12,000. But if four of
them have an annual income of $20,000, two of $10,000, and

four of $5,000, the average income of that area would still be $12,000. Therefore, in considering whether John Jones, a resident of the second area, feeds and clothes his family well, it makes no sense to say, "Since he is from an area where the average annual income per person is $12,000, he probably does." The *average* income of the area has nothing to do with Jones's income: He earns $5,000 per year. If we extended our definition of his area to include some millionaires in the next town, the average annual income might climb to $50,000 a year, but Jones would be no better off.

This is a grossly understated example, but it conveys the point of the ecological fallacy. Since averages, percentages, and correlation coefficients are used in quantitative methodologies, the possibility of committing the ecological fallacy is greatest here.

Reductionism, on the other hand, is more frequently encountered in qualitative research. Research of this type avoids numerical methods and relies instead upon the analyst's ability to "make sense" of situations and structures. Frequently this involves attempting to take the viewpoint of the actors involved in what is taking place. In other words, the analyst tries to understand some social phenomenon as it is understood by the actors engaged in it. Obviously such an approach is psychologistic; it attempts a subjective evaluation. So long as the analyst remains at this subjective level—that is, so long as he claims to be seeing the activity as the actor is seeing it—error may not be involved. If, however, he claims that in doing so he is really analyzing the collective, or group, action, then he is committing the error of reductionism. Groups, *as groups,* do not have feelings or perceptions; only individuals do. To attribute to some group phenomenon the properties of its members is to commit the fallacy of reductionism. It amounts to asserting that since $B_{12}$ is a triangle, B is a triangle.

Unfortunately, some adherents of both camps in American sociology, the quantitative methodologists and the qualitative methodologists, persist in arguing about which approach is "better." Such arguments make little sense. There are macrosocial phenomena that are best handled quantitatively: those involving large numbers of individuals, populations, survey research, theories involving probabilistic occurrences, and correlations between time-space phenomena, for example. And then there are many microsocial phenomena best handled qualitatively, such as those involving social definitions, deviance, lifestyles, and the like. The methodology one employs must be matched to the kind of research one is conducting, and to one's own intellectually challenged understanding of what society "is."

This kind of "matching" of method and problem occurs less often than one might suppose. As all students know, aptitude tests such as the SAT, the GRE, and the like disclose that most individuals have either quantitative or verbal skills, but seldom both. Sociology, however, draws upon both types of students. Hence, some sociologists can just about add, while others can just about spell. The former deride quantitative methods, which they are incapable of understanding, and the latter deride qualitative methods as metaphysical nonsense and therefore unscientific. The great debate on sociological research methods is no more complex than that.

It is important that the student employ whichever aptitude is strongest in himself and that he develop a tolerant attitude toward rival camps. American society is confronted with too many real problems for sociologists to waste time arguing about each other's aptitudes. The point of any research is to get involved to the maximum limit of one's intellectual ability, however that ability is inclined. Research must be personally meaningful. If the student is blessed with both quantitative and verbal aptitudes (as sometimes happens), then he is fortunate indeed; he has greater flexibility in matching the methodology to the problem than most of his colleagues have, and he may be able to check one methodology against another for maximum yield of information.

Quantitative and qualitative methods are really two sides of the same coin. The basic assumptions required in analysis are the same for both approaches, as we have seen in the previous examples. One can examine similarities and differences using highly complex statistical procedures or by means of verbal formulations. A bad mathematician who is a sociologist had better stick to verbal formulations, and a bad grammarian who is a sociologist had better be good at mathematics. The sociologist C. Wright Mills claimed that every sociologist should develop his own methodology, employing the best talents he has available.

An additional word of caution is required here. The mere fact of having passed required mathematics or English courses does not mean that one possesses sufficient mathematical or verbal ability to judge which single face of the coin, heads or tails, is "better" for all cases. No one—not even the foremost sociologist —can decide that. In order to make such an assertion, sociological theory must rest on a much firmer foundation than it does today. If we have "bad" methodology, of quantitative or qualitative varieties, it is because we have inherited a great deal of "bad" theory. Indeed, as noted previously, we have several conflicting *theories* but (thus far) no consistent set of *theory* such as that possessed by physics or biology. Until and unless we arrive at one, it is doubtful that our methodology can be standardized or the argument settled. This is well worth considering before attempting to take sides in the pointless quantitative *vs.* qualitative debate.

## Units of Analysis and Levels of Discourse

Our earlier discussion of the ecological and atomistic fallacies is related to a more general aspect of analysis. When we compared A and B, we were comparing two entities of the same kind or category: two geometric figures. Similarly, in comparing the works of Jonson and Shakespeare we were drawing samples from a common universe: the literary production of seventeenth-century England. While we may compare the life chances of white males in New York City with the life chances of white males in Alaska, it makes little sense to compare the life chances of white males anywhere with, let us say, the number of years the Third Reich lasted, or the size of the state of Texas. *Only things of the same kind can be compared.* Just as we would be in error were we to attribute properties of individuals to groups and vice versa, so we are in error whenever we mix our *units of analysis.* In conducting any type of comparison, we must always ask ourselves, "What is it I am comparing? What is my unit of analysis? Is it the individual, the group, the state, the city, or what?" And just as it is important to compare only things of the same kind, so, too, must we apply only the same scales to one as we do to the other. It would be foolish to measure the angles of A but the side lengths of B, and then compare A and B. Angles and lengths are not the same *level of measurement*. We may make comparisons between two or more objects or phenomena only if they are composed of the same units of analysis and only if the same scale is applicable to all of them. It is obviously impossible to compare the works of Jonson with the state of Kansas. Not only are these different units of analysis, but there is no common measure applicable to both.

Similarly, we may not compare an individual property with a group property, or a global property with either. This will be discussed in a later chapter.

## CONCEPTS, WORDS, AND PHENOMENA

Before leaving this introductory portion of the text, a few words must be added regarding conceptualization in general. The following discussion may be familiar to those with some background in logic or linguistic analysis, but is worth reconsidering; it is fundamental to all varieties of sociological research.

*Concepts* are mental products, communicated by the use of words and signs between individuals who share a common culture. A word or sign is a *symbol* of a concept. The study of man-made signs is called *semiotics*. The division of semiotics that deals with word signs is *semantics*. It may be difficult at first to think of words as nothing more nor less than signs, but it is less difficult to understand that the words we employ are useful only if they refer to concepts. When asked to define a word, the user of a language employs other words, hoping that the concepts communicated by these words will illuminate the concept intended by the word under consideration.

Except for nonsense words, words that have evolved in any language have meaning with respect to concepts: They have *conceptual meaning*; at least this appears to be true with respect to the *substantives,* the class of words that includes nouns and adjectives. The substantives denote objects, qualities, things, properties. There are other classes of words in a language. One class, composed of words such as "or," "and," "but," and "not," is used primarily for *logical operations* in linking together other words. The *verbs* designate activity, action, movement.

Suppose we consider the concept *weight*. The word *weight* is the sign in English for a particular concept that has evolved in many other languages as well, although these other languages do not substitute the same six-letter word for that concept as we do. The mental activity stimulated in English-speaking people by the word spelled w-e-i-g-h-t is a particular concept, and this concept is an abstraction of what we believe to be a common property of all physical objects in the external world. Of course, this concept has developed among people living on the surface of the earth, under particular conditions of observation. If individuals were born in earth-orbiting satellites under conditions of weightlessness, they probably would not have need for such a concept and would not evolve a word to denote it. Since the primary goal of language is communication between individuals sharing a common environment, language is reflective of that environment and the experiences and needs of its users. Because of the differences in history existing between separated communities, they have not all been subjected to the same collective experiences. Hence, particular concepts may be missing in some languages, and these languages will not contain the words to designate these concepts. It is often difficult to translate the precise meaning of a word in one language into the words of another language for this very reason.

Words are signs for concepts, and concepts are mental, not physical. Words, however, are composed of sounds, and take place in the physical world. By uttering these arrangements of sounds (or *phonemes*), one individual signals to another some commonly shared mental notion or picture.

But what are all these sounds and concepts about? In discussing the concept *weight*, we mentioned that it was an abstraction from physical reality concerning some common property of all objects and physical things. There are, then, objects, things, activities, actions, processes, and the like going on in the physical world—or at least *believed* to be going on in the physical world by the language community employing the words—that makes such concepts possible and also makes possible the creation of words to denote them. What goes on external to the mental world, in the world of physical reality that the mental must deal with, are *phenomena*.

Thus, external to the observer are the *phenomena* taking place in the physical world; within the mind of the observer are concepts denoting these phenomena; and communication between minds takes place in the form of words signifying these concepts. Hence, words serve as mediators between the world of objective, external reality and the internal, subjective world of the mind.

This raises several problems. It is obvious that something does not exist in external, objective reality simply because we have a word and concept for it. *Mermaid* is an English word denoting a concept, that of a creature half-fish, half-woman; but we can agree that no object exists in the external world corresponding to this concept. There are many words such as *mermaid* that have been inherited from the past and reflect beliefs about objective reality no longer shared by the community employing the language. Thus there are words corresponding to concepts for which no phenomena exist. What is a *glosk*? Nothing; I have invented the word. No concept is signified by it. Nonsense words exist for which there are not only no external phenomena but no concepts corresponding to them. Since a great deal of socialization takes place in the form of language, much of what we believe about objective reality is based upon what has been communicated to us in the form of words, and not all words are equally legitimate, in the sense that not all words denote concepts corresponding to phenomena. To compound the problem further, most, if not all, of our thought processes take place in the form of words; worse yet, many philosophers, particularly among the ancients, did not distinguish between words, concepts, and external phenomena. They believed that the exterior world was governed by the laws of their native grammar, and the logic they invented was really a disguised form of rhetoric. They sat indoors arguing about the world outside the walls of the academy, without ever venturing forth to engage the world by testing their assumptions by the events themselves.

Concepts are mental. But the phenomena they designate are objects and activities having form and (in the case of objects) substance. Of course, using nothing but words, one could argue, via the rules of grammar and syntax of language, that even *phenomena* may be mental. Is all reality only a product of my mind?

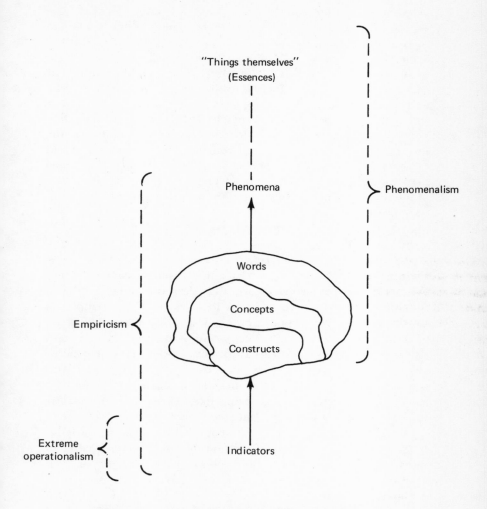

Figure 1-4.  The place of concepts in social research.

It may be that I am the only thing existing. Employing nothing but language and logic, I could argue that nothing takes place or *is* when *I* am not there. This argument is a variant of the old "Does a tree falling in the forest make a noise when no one is there?" question with which the student is certainly familiar. Some excellent minds of the past have argued that there is no reality other than that of the *mental self.* It should be apparent that I, for one, do not subscribe to this notion, or I would not be writing this text. I am writing this text because I believe that *you* and others like you (and myself) will be reading this when *not* in my presence. Thus, I do not subscribe to *solipsism,* the belief that "I alone exist." I am convinced that there is a world external to myself, where *you* exist, which words and concepts may not adequately describe, but which is experienced by others of my own kind in a manner very similar, if not identical, to my own experiences.

Just as *concepts* are *words,* so, too, *constructs* are *concepts.* In terms of set theory, the *universe of words* includes the set *concepts,* and within the set *concepts* is the subset *constructs* (see Figure 1–4). A construct is a consciously invented concept rather than one that has evolved naturally. Very often the word employed to designate a construct is identical with that employed for the concept. For example, one may speak of a friend as being of a certain "class." The concept *class* is older than sociology. But in sociology the construct *class* means more than the concept *class* means in ordinary usage. In sociology it is connected with other constructs, such as life chance and life-style, socio-economic status, social stratification, and the like. An example frequently used to distinguish *concept* and *construct* is the word *intelligence.* Intelligence is a concept that evolved with the English language as an expression of an abstract and innate quality of individuals. *In the social sciences the concept "intelligence" is used as a construct.* For one thing, we have devised *indicators* (standardized scales) for measuring it. When we refer to *intelligence* at the level of the construct, we are referring to a property of the individual that we believe is measurable in a certain way. This may not quite agree with the general usage of the word-concept *intelligence.* It may be that the construct applies to a sociocultural property of the individual, not to an innate property of his genetic make-up. It may be that what English-speaking people generally mean by their concept is not what we mean by our construct. Our construct relates to one's ability to perform on a certain kind of test; it may be unrelated to what the concept means in ordinary usage. But we know how our construct relates to other constructs we employ, and we prefer to define these in ways that tend to make them less ambiguous than they are in everyday language. In everday language one concept may mean many different things and one word may stand for many concepts; *mass,* for example, means the quality of size and weight, a Christian religious ceremony, the main or principal part, and the like. In physics it means only the quantity of matter in a body as measured in relation to its inertia. This last is at the level of constructs. Everyday usages are concepts, the relations between them being somewhat obscure. To escape the obscurity of everyday language, science employs constructs.

In general, constructs are formed by usage and mutual agreement within scholarly communities: It is understood that the word designates a particular property, or category. It may or may not be interchangeable with the concept employed in everyday speech. Most academic disciplines have specific areas of inquiry and have developed their own nomenclatures for treating them. Sociological "jargon" is composed primarily of constructs, and this causes a certain confusion in the minds of the lay public, who tend to believe that we misunderstand what their words *really* mean!

*Indicators,* as already noted, are standardized scales for measuring concepts. An I.Q. test is an indicator useful for measuring the construct *intelligence.* A ruler and protractor are indicators useful for measuring linear size and angles of plane figures, as we saw in the case of Figure 1–1. Income, education, and occupation are useful *indicators* of the socio-economic status of individuals.

What we call "reality" is not neatly constructed, and what is "real" or "not real" is a subject of contention in Western philosophical systems, and between peoples of different cultures. Just as I do not hold to solipsism, so I do not hold to *monism,* the notion that the objects of the world and our ideas of them—that is, our mental notions of them—are one and the same. I am also too much of a scientist to be persuaded by *metaphysical* arguments: those about matters that cannot be verified in human experience or *demonstrated* to be true. Whether there exists something beyond the phenomenon—a "thing in itself," with its own peculiar *essence,* such as an ideal triangle, which need not exist in time and space but has a special kind of existence—is intellectually interesting but perhaps irrelevant to our immediate tasks. Plato's "world of ideas," distinct and apart from experience, does not lend itself to scientific testing. This does not mean that it has no value; it simply lacks accessibility to empirical methods.

In Figure 1–4, I have indicated a few of the approaches to an understanding of reality that the student may encounter in his reading. Each has a theoretical base in philosophy, since each deals with meanings. Scientific *empiricism* attempts to measure, by means of indicators, constructs, and concepts, the phenomena of the world about us. It seeks to escape the "tyranny of words" by examining the relationships it finds between its indicators and relating these, in turn, to the observed phenomena. Extreme *operationalism* (or extreme *positivism*) insists that only the indicators and the relationships between them are "real." *Phenomenology* attempts to determine the essences lying within the subjective act of cognition and does not usually descend to any level lower than that of the concept. Some of its methods have been borrowed by ethnomethodology, which does, however, descend at least to the level of constructs. Ethnomethods aim primarily at descriptive accounts, which purport to reflect the view of reality obtained by participants engaged in what to them is social activity. These sometimes include *ethnographies,* descriptive accounts such as those furnished by anthropologists in attempting to describe the everyday, taken-for-granted organization and activity of tribes, clans, and the like. All these distinctions will mean more to the student as he himself becomes involved in applying different methods to different problems. They are mentioned here only as a kind of warning of the troubled waters lying immediately ahead. Meaning is more than skin-deep: We must dig for it, and there is no one method but a plurality of methods available to us.

*Operationalization* is the act of providing definitions, for use as indicators, that involve specifying how the construct or concept is to be measured. We will discuss this further in Chapter 2.

SUGGESTED READINGS

Bartholomew, D. J., and E. E. Bassett, *Let's Look at the Figures* (Baltimore: Penguin, 1971).

Denzin, Norman K. (ed.), *Sociological Methods: A Sourcebook* (Chicago, Aldine, 1970).

Dewey, John, *Logic: The Theory of Inquiry* (New York: Holt, Rinehart & Winston, 1938).

Lofland, John, *Analyzing Social Settings* (Belmont, Calif.: Wadsworth, 1972).

Madge, John, *Origins of Scientific Sociology* (New York: Free Press, 1962).

Mead, George Herbert, *Mind, Self and Society* (Chicago: University of Chicago Press, 1934).

Russell, Bertrand, *Human Knowledge: Its Scope and Limits* (New York: Simon & Schuster, 1967).

Tufte, Edward R., *The Quantitative Analysis of Social Problems* (Reading, Mass.: Addison-Wesley, 1970).

# II

# Some Principal
# Methods

# 2

# *Content Analysis*

Now that the student has some idea of the kinds of traps he may fall into by misuse of research methods, he may proceed to learn. Perhaps the easiest method to begin with is the set of techniques collectively known as "content analysis."

Content analysis may be defined as a methodology by which the researcher seeks to determine the manifest content of written, spoken, or published communications by *systematic, objective,* and *quantitative* analysis. It is, then, a quantitative method applicable to what has traditionally been called qualitative material—written language. The techniques that comprise this method have been developed by sociologists, psychologists, linguists, political analysts, and others. Since any written communication (and this includes novels, plays, and television scripts as well as personal letters, suicide notes, magazines, and newspaper accounts) is produced by a communicator, the *intention of the communicator* may be the object of our research. Or we may be interested in the audience, or *receiver* of the communication, and may attempt to determine something about it. For example, since popular literature is responsive to the taste of its audience, we may wish to determine what this taste is, or was at a specified period. Content-analysis techniques have been employed by psychologists in efforts to determine personality traits of individuals.

They have been used in propaganda analysis, in children's readers to reveal sex-role stereotyping to measure trends in dating practices or in audience and consumer interests, and to determine who wrote what and when.

In more elaborate versions, content analysis is used by government agencies to monitor changes in the attitudes of friendly and hostile nations and by political parties to determine subtle changes in opposition "party lines."

In its most elementary form, it may consist solely of counting the number of times a particular word is used and comparing this with a count of other words in the same document. For example, suppose that after reading a political speech several times we are still uncertain of the speaker's position regarding some pending legislation. We might count the number of times he says something favorable about the particular bill and compare it with the number of times he says something unfavorable. If we add the total of these two counts we obtain the total number of references made by him to the bill. We could then compare the two counts and reach a conclusion on his position. Or we could total the references, dividing the result into the number of favorable references and multiplying this by 100 to obtain the percentage of favorable references. The degree to which this differs from 50 percent tells us whether he is for or against the bill, and the magnitude of his support as well. That is, if the result is less than 50 percent, we may infer that he is against the bill; if more than 50 percent, that he is for it. If the result is very much more (or less) than 50 percent, he is obviously strongly for (or against) the bill.

Of course, if he were very strongly for the bill it should have been obvious without performing the content analysis in the first place. This is an important point to remember. Since content analysis always involves counting, and with lengthy documents this can grow tedious, it should not be used if the expected results are readily apparent.

Another point. Notice how easily I slipped into error with my explanation above. I should have stated a hypothesis, something like: "Senator X is for the bill." Then, if the actual count were to come up to greater than 50 percent positive, I would be *unable to reject* the hypothesis that he is for the bill. If it came out less than 50 percent I would have to reject the hypothesis.

In this example we would go through the speech and whenever we found a *pro* reference to the bill, mark a plus sign above it; for an *anti* reference, we would mark a minus sign. But what is to be considered a "reference"? That is, what is to be the *scoring unit?* Is it a word, a phrase, a clause, a sentence, or a paragraph? This must be decided prior to performing the actual scoring of plus and minus. Probably the safest method is to include as one unit the minimum number of words containing a whole meaning. Thus, in a sentence from the works of Mao Tse-tung:

> Our cultural workers must serve the people with great enthusiasm and devotion

the meaning units have been underlined. Sometimes, a meaning unit consists of only one word, sometimes of two ("cultural workers") or three ("serve the people").

Although we are going to tally the number of such meaning units having positive affect, we must not confuse these with our *unit of analysis,* that which we are analyzing. In the present case, our unit of analysis is *the speech.* If we were comparing two speeches or six the unit of analysis would still be *the speech.* Of course, we might be interested in comparing different pages of the speech, to see whether the expressed attitude undergoes change; in that case, the unit of analysis is *the page,* although the scoring unit may remain the meaning unit.

Book, speech,
document, etc.

| | |
|---|---|
| pages | If we score pages and compare books, the *scoring unit* is the page, the *unit of analysis* is the book. |
| paragraphs | If we score paragraphs and compare pages, the *scoring unit* is the paragraph, the *unit of analysis* |
| sentences | is the page. |
| phrases | We could, of course, score paragraphs and compare books, or score clauses and compare books, |
| clauses | |
| meaning units | etc. |
| (words) | |

Notice that in evaluating a speech by scoring the meaning units within it, we are not committing the atomistic fallacy. A speech has no existence apart from the sequence of words within it. A speech is unlike a group, in which membership may change but the group persist, because changing the words in a speech—the "membership"—makes it a *different* speech.

To clarify the matter of scoring, consider the following example from a hypothetical political speech:

I dislike equanimity. One must take sides, particularly on such an

    – a              A            A              – a
unpopular issue as this one. While passage of the bill is sure to cause

          – a
distress among many loyal citizens . . .

Here the meaning units have been underlined. To continue our earlier example, we have decided to test the hypothesis that Senator X (the speaker) is *for* the bill. Wherever any meaning unit includes the word *bill* or a substitute for it, we identify the meaning unit with an "A." Any phrase or adjective having "A" as its object or subject, or modifying "A," is given an "a" to identify it. Those "a's" having negative affect, or feeling, are scored with a minus sign; those having a positive affect, or feeling, with a plus sign. Hence, words in a meaning unit such as "love" or "like" would make the meaning unit plus or positive; "hate" and "dislike" would make the meaning unit negative. We could go through the entire speech, marking each meaning unit referring to the bill either plus or minus. Then, as mentioned before, we would total the number of scored units and divide the total into the number of plus units; this gives us a decimal, or *proportion*; multiplying this by 100 gives us the percentage of positive references of the total references to the bill:

$$\frac{\text{sum of positive units}}{\text{sum of positive and negative units}} = \text{proportion} \times 100 = \%\text{positive}$$

The student should be wary of attributed sentiments, which may have different values in different contexts. The last meaning unit in the sample, "many loyal citizens," could ordinarily be scored positive; here, coupled to the negative affective "distress," it must be scored negative. To "cause distress" to the "enemy" is a positive evaluation; to "cause distress" to "loyal citizens," however, is a negative evaluation and should be so scored.

## CATEGORIES

In the example given, we were attempting to evaluate only one category, the attitude of the speaker toward the bill. Usually we are interested in more than one category. In a speech or political document, we might be interested, for example, in comparing the total number of references to domestic affairs with the total number of references to foreign affairs. Here we have two *categories* to be scored, or tallied. As a matter of fact, since content analysis involves scoring an entire document or group of documents, it is seldom performed when only a single category is to be evaluated; it is too time-consuming for such slim information.

Suppose we had available several hundred suicide notes, left by victims of successful acts of suicide. After reading them through several times, we may be able to hypothesize that suicides generally attempt to implicate some other person in their act. Perhaps a lover, husband or wife, friend, or parent is most frequently cited. But does this other person play only a passive role? If the answer to such questions is not apparent from repeated readings, we may decide to undertake a content analysis of all the notes. Before we do so, however, we should make a *research design,* spelling out what we are attempting to show and how we plan to go about doing it. The design must clearly specify the hypotheses to be tested and the categories to be scored. This is true of almost all sociological methods; we do not enter upon "fishing trips," hoping that something will turn up in the data that will make the excursion worthwhile.

Any sociological investigation must begin by defining a problem in terms of categories.* These categories must reflect the purpose of the research. We begin by asking ourselves what it is we propose to test. In our first example, it was the attitude of the speaker, Senator X, toward the bill. At the phenomenal level

* The discussion here is indebted to chap. 5 of Ole R. Holsti's *Content Analysis for the Social Sciences and Humanities* (Reading, Mass.: Addison-Wesley, 1969).

(of Figure 2–4) this is a propensity for action that is a property of Senator X. This property is generalized in English by the concept *attitude*. As *indicators* of that concept we used meaning units having that concept as subject or object. We ignored other meaning units. We were able to do so only because we had provided ourselves with an *operational definition* of the category to be scored. What we actually did was agree to score *only those meaning units having a positive or negative affect and the concept as subject or object, and to score each such unit only once in polarity.* Thus we defined the category to be scored in terms of operations to be performed. This excludes many other categories: Ideally, it should exclude all other categories.

If we had been scoring a document in terms of the number of references to domestic affairs and foreign affairs and had hypothesized a relationship between them, then we would have had to provide operational definitions of each of these categories. In providing such definitions, it is important that they be so phrased that their meanings do not overlap. In fact, the first principle of categorization in social-science methodology is that *categories must be mutually exclusive.* Any scored unit must fall unequivocally into one category and no more than one.

In addition, *categories must be exhaustive.* That is, they must be so formed that they are capable of including within the set of them all possible cases to be examined. The reasons for this are apparent. By keeping categories conceptually clean, ambiguity in meaning is reduced and more logical conclusions may be reached. In addition, reliability is improved, since another person, armed with these categories, is more likely to arrive at the same results. Indeed, comparing the independent scorings of several scorers of the same data is a direct measure of reliability.

The mutual-exclusion and exhaustive principles must be met before any inference or deduction may be drawn from category analysis. In sampling the population of the Southwest, for example, it would make little sense to include "white persons" and "black persons" as the only categories. These categories are not exhaustive: Indians, Chicanos, Orientals, and so on are omitted. "Whites/nonwhites" is exhaustive, or "Indians/non-Indians," since "non" includes all others than those specified. Whether one breaks the sampled population into two such parts and, if so, how one makes the division are related to the research problem defined. If one were looking for the distribution of income or life chances as a function of ethnic origin, it would be necessary to include, as separate categories, every possible ethnic variety found in the area. If one is trying to discover the distribution of ascribed qualities as a function of non-European ethnic origin, only two categories are required. Whatever the problem under consideration, the categories established by the researcher must reflect all possibilities and be nonoverlapping.

## VARIABLES

This brings us directly to the subject of variables. Concepts may be either constants or variables. A constant has only one value and is fixed. Variables, on the other hand, are capable of assuming more than one value. In our example, we treated the concept *attitude* as a *dichotomous variable*. A dichotomy is a division into two parts, such as "good/bad"; it makes no allowances for variations in between. It is therefore *bipolar,* having only two poles. "Hot/cold," for example, divides the concept *temperature* in two. It is a simple scale for measuring the state of the variable *temperature.* "Hot/warm/tepid/cool/cold" is another scale for measuring this variable. It is somewhat more precise than the dichotomous variable but unfortunately does not clearly specify the degree of difference between the units. It is not clear, for example, whether "hot" differs from "warm" to the same extent that "warm" differs from "tepid," or "cold" from "cool." Such scales of varying intensity without equal divisions between their units are called *ordinal scales.* The Fahrenheit and centigrade scales, on the other hand, are *interval scales,* on which the difference between units is the same throughout; adding one degree or subtracting one degree is possible at any value and has the same meaning no matter what the starting point.

In treating attitude as a dichotomous variable, we are making no allowance for the intensity of feeling contained in the meaning units. Each scoring unit is marked either plus or minus if it refers to the bill. If the speaker says "good," his remark receives the same score as if he had said "best" or "greatest." This compromises the accuracy of the results somewhat. Scoring accuracy could be improved if, instead of treating attitude as a dichotomous variable, we employed a scale of varying intensity or *potency,* such as an ordinal or interval scale, which could take such differences into account. Then, when the adjective "best" appeared in a meaning unit, it could be rated higher than, say, "good." We would still be attempting to measure along the same dimension—feeling for or against the bill—but we could express this dimension in finer gradations than a simple plus or minus.

If we wanted even greater accuracy, we could add more dimensions to be scored instead of just dividing our one dimension into finer gradations. Charles Osgood and his associates * have discovered, through an analysis of English words, that almost all involve three dimensions of meaning: *evaluation* (such as our "good" or "bad"), *potency* (the intensity of the evaluation), and *activity* (the degree of motion conveyed). Their method of word analysis, called the *semantic differential,* is extensively used in survey research but is amenable to content-analysis research as well.

From the foregoing it is evident that we may use one scale or many scales, one dimension or more, and various scoring units in the measurement of meanings. The categories selected must be kept conceptually clean, nonoverlapping, and all-inclusive. A research design must be formulated prior to any research, and it should spell out the hypothesis relating concepts, the indicators of these concepts that will be employed, and operationalized definitions enabling the researcher to recognize a unit to be scored when he finds one. Data collection then follows; this involves scoring according to the operationalized definitions in the research design. After all scoring is performed, data analysis begins.

## RESULTS OF ANALYSIS

Results may be presented in the form of graphs, tables, numbers, or mathematical (statistical) tests. If the student has taken a course in elementary social statistics, he is here advised that nonparametric tests are most applicable to the results of content analysis, since these measure the internal distribution of properties of the sample. In most cases, it will not be possible to

* Charles Osgood *et al., The Measurement of Meaning* (Urbana: University of Illinois Press, 1957).

infer from these internal properties some quality or property of the *population* rather than of the *sample*. Warnings to this effect are found in all texts where nonparametric statistical tests are discussed and will not be elaborated upon here.

Aside from statistical tests, results may be presented as proportions, percentages, bar graphs, or other graphic representations. If we found that 62 percent of the references to the bill were negative, for example, we might represent our findings in any of the forms shown in Figure 2–1.

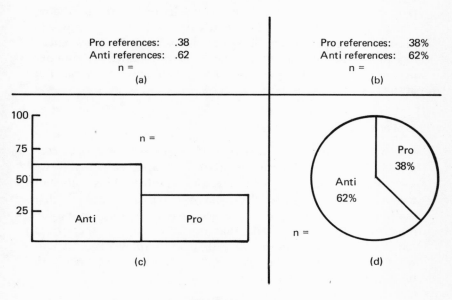

**Figure 2-1**

Figure 2–1a gives results as *proportions* of the total number of units scored, 2–1b as *percentages*, 2–1c as a *histogram*, and 2–1d as a *sector graph*. On the basis of the results, one must decide whether to reject or fail to reject the hypothesis of the research design. If the researcher has statistical methods at his disposal, he should be able to show the statistical *level of confidence* he has in making this decision.

Whatever method of presentation is employed, the total number of units score, $n$, should always be shown. If 580 units of analysis were scored, then $n = 580$. With respect to Figure 2–1c, the *ordinate* (the upright leg of the graph) may show either *frequency* (number of units) or *percentage of total,* and the choice should be indicated. In other words, the graph of Figure 2–1c is meaningless as shown, for the reader has no way of knowing whether the numbers listed on the left are percentages or units of analysis. Figure 2–1c should be changed; the ordinate should have its increments identified.

Since there are various approaches to content analysis, any report made by the researcher should specify the techniques employed, the categories scored, the reliability obtained, and the research hypothesis as well as the results. Reliability may be expressed as the percentage of agreement between the researcher's scoring of the document and the scoring obtained by another person employing the same categories. In student work it may not always be possible to have another scoring.

## INDEPENDENT AND DEPENDENT VARIABLES

In most sociological research we attempt to show some connection between one form of activity and another. That is, we show that one activity *correlates* with another. This does not mean that the one causes the other. What it does mean is that the one is found alongside the other—that if the one occurs, the other is likely to occur—and that the occurrence of the two is somehow related. Remembering that we employ concepts corresponding to observable activities or properties, we may wish to assert, for example, that

X ————————▶ Y

This assertion means that concept X implies concept Y, or that the presence of X is associated with the presence of Y. Once again, we are not asserting that X causes Y; causality is virtually impossible to prove. The concept X is referred to as the *independent variable* and Y as the *dependent variable.* This is due to the fact that, in our research, we vary X and observe what happens to Y; Y is *dependent* upon X, but X is assumed to be nondependent on, or independent of, Y, at least so far as our research hypothesis is concerned. What we are asking in our research is, "If I change X, what do I observe in Y? If I increase X, does Y increase? Does it decrease? Does it remain constant?" If we assume, in our research design, that an increase in Y goes with an increase in X, then we have assumed a *positive relationship* between the two variables:

Similarly, in a positive relationship between the variables X and Y, a decrease in Y should accompany a decrease in X.

If we assume in our research design that a *decrease* in Y accompanies an *increase* in X (or that an *increase* in Y accompanies a *decrease* in X), then we have specified a *negative relationship* between the two variables:

The arrow shows the *direction* of the relationship, from independent to dependent; the sign is its direct (*positive*) or inverse (*negative*) character. Hence, to say that X and Y are in *direct relationship* to each other is to say that if X increases, Y increases, and vice versa; to say that Y varies inversely with X is to say that as X goes up in value, Y goes down, or that as X goes down, Y goes up.

RESEARCH DESIGN

As we have seen, content analysis may be employed to measure an attitude toward a topic, such as the passage of a bill. The same senator's voting record on, let us say, welfare legislation is available in the *Congressional Record*. Is there a correlation between two separate activities of senators, such as their attitude toward supporting intervention in Southeast Asia and their support of welfare legislation? We see the start of a research design to test such a possible correlation. Figure 2–2 is one form the research design might take.

In Figure 2–2, the two variables, X and Y, are hypothesized to have a negative relationship. If X is large, we expect Y to

*Research Hypothesis:* The greater a senator's support of intervention in Southeast Asia (independent variable), the less his support of welfare legislation (dependent variable).

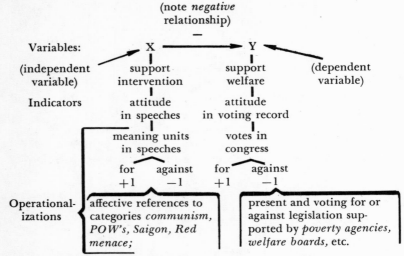

*Sample:* All U.S. senators in period 1960–70; 10 speeches, 10 bills for each senator.

*Unit of analysis:* Expressed attitudes. Once these are tallied for each senator, similarities and differences among senators will be evaluated using contingency tables.

*Scoring units for content-analysis portion* (i.e., speeches): The *speech, net affect,* +1 or −1 (for or against), obtained by scoring *meaning units* + or − and adding the negative and positive sums obtained per speech. If sum per speech is from zero to some negative value, score speech −1; if sum per speech is some positive value, score speech +1.

(Tabulate an *intervention score* and a *welfare-support score* for each senator.)

Figure 2–2. A research design as it might be sketched out prior to undertaking the research.

be small; if X is small, we expect Y to be large. We expect, in other words, that those senators who support welfare legislation will be opposed to military intervention in Southeast Asia, and that those who oppose welfare legislation will support such intervention. Hence, we expect that the variables stand in inverse relation to one another.

In our design we have decided, for the sake of economy, to count each speech as either +1 (for intervention) or −1 (against intervention), and to base this decision on the *net* effect of the speech, derived by adding together the number of positive and negative scored meaning units within the speech. Such decisions are wholly up to the researcher. He must have the concepts that he seeks to evaluate clearly in mind. Since it is the attitude in each speech that interests him, and the attitude is the property of a senator, he wishes to compare the senators' attitudes by the net effect of their speeches. Ultimately, he wishes to compare two properties: *attitude toward intervention* and *attitude toward welfare legislation.* These are two distinct concepts each of which is conceived as a property of the same senator. Then, by comparing these two properties for all senators in the 1960–70 period, he hopes to determine whether there is a relationship between these properties and, if so, the character of that relationship. He has hypothesized that it has a negative or inverse character, but he cannot be sure of this without making observations of these properties for a representative sample of senators.

To measure the dependent variable Y, *attitude toward welfare,* we will score each senator's voting record +1 or −1 on each of ten pieces of legislation supported by poverty agencies, welfare boards, and the like. Since we are taking Y from the *Congressional Record* in the form of votes *for* and *against,* it probably does not seem to the reader that we are indeed performing content analysis on this half of the research design. Indeed, some might consider this part of the measuring as survey research, which we shall cover in Chapter 3. It is, however, a variety of content analysis, since we are evaluating documents (the *Congressional Record*) and attempting to make a measurement of a property (the *attitude* of senators toward welfare) not immediately apparent from a casual look at the record.

We may consider that each senator has an *intervention score* and a *welfare support* score, represented by what we obtain for each of the variables on the basis of his voting record and speeches. His intervention score can run from −10 to +10, since we are proposing to score ten speeches per senator. Similarly, since we are scoring ten of his votes for or against welfare legislation, we may have a welfare score running from $-10$ to $+10$ for each senator. Note that we decided to assign a score of $-1$ to all scores from zero to some negative value rather than simply to all negative values. Had we not scored zero as negative, our categories would not have been exhaustive, for had a senator obtained a net score of zero we would not have been able to assign him to the *against* or *for* categories.

In performing the content analysis and tallying the votes for each senator, we may construct a *raw data* matrix, or table, to keep track of things, such as that shown in Figure 2–3. In

| 1. Senator | 2. Intervention score | 3. Welfare score | 4. X | 5 Y | 6. x | 7. y |
|---|---|---|---|---|---|---|
| $Z_{11}$ | $+8$ | $+3$ | $+1$ | $+1$ | for | for |
| $Z_{12}$ | $+8$ | $-3$ | $+1$ | $-1$ | for | against |
| $Z_{13}$ | $+4$ | $-4$ | $+1$ | $-1$ | for | against |
| $Z_{14}$ | $-8$ | $+5$ | $-1$ | $+1$ | against | for |
| $Z_{15}$ | $-5$ | $-5$ | $-1$ | $-1$ | against | against |
| etc. | . . . . | . . . . | . . . . | . . . . | . . . . | . . . . |

Figure 2–3.　Raw-data table.

this table, each senator has been given a code number $Z$ for identification. It is best to write the name corresponding to this code elsewhere, before doing the final analysis of results, for the sake of objectivity. The *net* score obtained from his ten speeches is entered in column 2; the *net* score obtained from his ten votes in Congress is entered in column 3. Columns 4 and 5, which may be omitted if desired, merely translate the score in columns 2 and 3 into a $+1$ if the net score is positive or a $-1$ if the net score is negative. Similarly, columns 6 and 7 merely translate the $+1$ or $-1$ of columns 4 and 5 into "for" or "against" inferences. This could have been done directly from columns 2 and 3, but it is a good idea to keep track of every logical operation made in performing the data reduction.

Once we have entered the data from the content-analysis and voting record for all the senators in the period 1960–70, we can perform additional reductions of the data in order to analyze our findings. If we have tested 50 senators, we will have 100 scores: 50 for X and 50 for Y. Each senator has a score on X and a score on Y in our raw-data table. Some will be found to support intervention but not welfare, others will support both, some neither, and some will support welfare but not intervention. How can we sort these out in such a way that similarities and differences are immediately apparent?

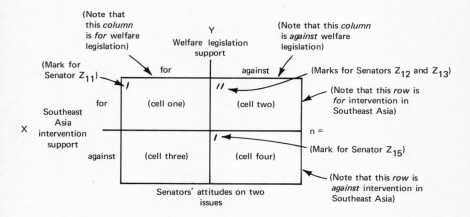

Figure 2-4. Constructing a contingency table.

The simplest and most direct way to do this is to use a four-celled *contingency table,* of the type shown in Figure 2–4. We construct this table by considering our two variables, X and Y. Each variable has two possibilities, "for" and "against," as shown in our raw-data table, columns 6 and 7.

Consider Senator $Z_{11}$ first. He is *for* intervention and *for* welfare. We check him off our raw-data table and enter a mark for him in cell 1 of our contingency table, since this cell is for those who are *for* on X and *for* on Y. Our second senator, $Z_{12}$, is *for* intervention (X) but *against* welfare legislation (Y). We make a mark for him in cell 2, since this cell is for those who are *for* X but *against* Y. $Z_{13}$ is also *for* intervention but *against* welfare, so he goes into cell 2 as well. We proceed down

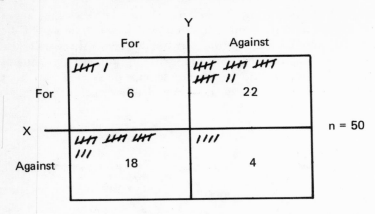

Figure 2-5. The contingency table of the previous figure, with all data from the raw-data table inserted and tab marks changed to numerals.

our raw-data table in this way, checking off each senator and making a mark for him in the appropriate cell. Senator $Z_{15}$, for example, is *against* X and *against* Y: We would make a mark for him in cell 4. As the scores mount up in each cell, we cross four marks with our fifth mark, as if we were keeping tabs in a counting operation. Since we have an appropriate cell for each possible combination of *for* and *against* that can occur, when we have checked off all 50 senators on our raw-data table the total number of marks in all four cells of our contingency table should equal 50. If it does not, we will have to return to the data table and recheck what we have done. When we are satisfied that each of the 50 senators has been assigned to the correct cell, we can place a number in each cell corresponding to the number of marks made in that cell. Our results may look something like Figure 2–5.

We see that we have 28 senators *for* intervention in Southeast Asia (6 + 22) and 22 *against* it (18 + 4). Also, we have 24 *for* welfare legislation (6 + 18) but 26 against it (22 + 4). However, the most significant information is obtained from contingency tables by looking at the *diagonals,* not at the rows and columns.

The first question to ask is "Which diagonal contains most of the cases?" In this case, it is the diagonal rising from left to right (from cell 3 to cell 2). This tells us at once that there is *a negative relationship between X and Y.* Had the other diagonal, that running from cell 1 to cell 4, contained most of the cases, it would have denoted a positive relationship between X and Y. In other words, most of those for X would have been for Y, and those against X would have been against Y. But this did not occur. Instead, the large number in cell 3 tells us that a large number of senators who were against X were for Y, and the large number in cell 2 tells us that a large number of senators who were for X were against Y.

We had hypothesized that the greater a senator's support of intervention in Southeast Asia, the less he would support welfare legislation. We had thus hypothesized a negative relationship between our two variables, X and Y. Our contingency table reveals just such a negative relationship between X and Y. Hence, we cannot reject the hypothesis and should be very pleased that our results turned out this way.

Our contingency table also shows that the relationship between the two variables is not a perfect one; the inverse relationship is true of most, but not all, of the senators in our

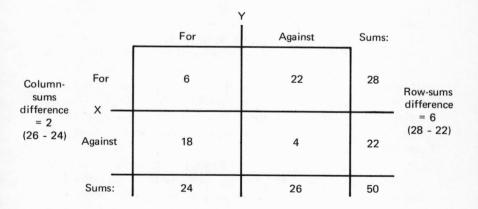

Figure 2-6. Examining the marginals.

sample. We can best see this by summing the rows and then summing the columns in our example, as in Figure 2–6. We can place these sums at the margins or sides of our table. These sums are referred to as *marginals*. Marginals show the internal distribution of the data; in this case, we see that the internal distribution is not uniform. The difference between column sums is not the same as the difference between row sums. In other words, the difference between rows is not the same as the difference between columns. Here we are performing the same operation we did in Chapter 1 with A and B of Figure 1–3. Note, too, that the difference within rows is not the same (18 − 4 = 14, but 22 − 6 = 16), nor within columns. Some additional influence is at work here, but what this is cannot be determined by our data in the form in which we have them. Actually, we should have *controlled* for other factors, such as the political party of the senators. Perhaps the relationship holds more uniformly for Republican senators than for Democratic ones. Or perhaps it is influenced by the geographical region the senator represents. In more exact research, we would obtain such information as political party and record it along with our other data and see whether it affects the results we obtain.

Figure 2–7 shows some of the other possible results we might have obtained. Figure 2–7a also shows a negative relationship, but notice that is a weaker relationship than that of Figure 2–6. It is weaker, since the difference between the diagonals is less pronounced than in Figure 2–6. In Figure 2–7b, the relationship has become so weak that it has disappeared! Here there is no correlation between the strength of X and that of Y, and therefore no relationship exists. If we had obtained this result, we would have to reject our hypothesis. In Figure 2–7c, the relationship is in the positive direction. Here, too, we would have to reject our hypothesis, since our results show the opposite of what we had predicted.

Contingency tables provide a simple analytical tool for determining whether a relationship exists and, if so, its direction, strength, and the presence of contaminating variables. It is the most widely used device in social research because of its simplicity of form and its ability to show so much information.

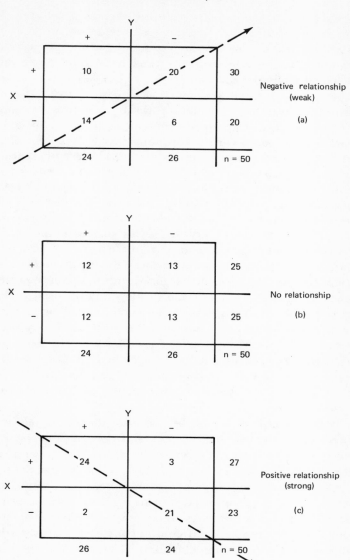

Figure 2-7. Some examples of contingency tables that could have resulted from the research (+ = for, − = against). See Figure 2-6.

## VARIETIES OF CONTENT ANALYSIS

The researcher should always consider possible applications of content-analysis techniques to subject areas of interest to him. The possibilities are unlimited.

The great Russian-American sociologist Pitirim Sorokin classified paintings of various periods into two categories, *religious* and *secular,* in an attempt to learn when changes in the world view had occurred. He found that 94.7 percent of the known European paintings of the tenth and eleventh centuries were of a religious nature and only 5.3 percent were secular. By the fourteenth and fifteenth centuries, the percentage of paintings of a religious nature had dropped to 85, by the seventeenth century to 50.2, by the nineteenth century to 10, and by the twentieth century to 3, with corresponding rises in the secular category. This is an example of content analysis of nonverbal materials. It is also typical of *trend analysis,* the attempt to find differences in categories with the passage of time. Thus it is particularly applicable to the study of social change. One could present such data as Sorokin's plotted on a graph, with the centuries on the horizontal axis (the *abscissa*) and the percentages on the vertical axis (the *ordinate*). (This technique is discussed further in Chapter 7.) Note that Sorokin's two categories are mutually exclusive and exhaustive: Any painting not falling into the religious category must fall into the secular category.

This same technique may be used for themes of television serials, movies, plays, and magazines. In a previous book, I utilized sets of categories to show the differences between the themes of Shakespeare's plays and those of his contemporaries. My purpose was to uncover persisting patterns of group inter-action that retain their social structuring across the centuries, although the social meanings associated with them may have undergone change. The social group of three persons (the triad) contains certain persisting structural elements, but these are not always interpreted in the same way.

Propaganda techniques may be studied by scoring the frequency of occurrence of guilt by association, name-calling, oversimplification, glittering generalities, and related categories. An excellent bibliography of what has been done, together with many examples of how to do it, is included in Ole Holsti's *Content Analysis for the Social Sciences and Humanities* (Boston, Mass.: Addison-Wesley, 1969).

It is important in content analysis to begin with a definition of the problem in the form of a hypothesis to be tested. It is best to write out the hypothesis, preferably in terms of two or more variables with the relationship between them specified. Remember that these variables are concepts and should be operationalized in such a way that they are measurable by some method of enumeration. The categories to be scored must serve as indicators for these concepts. These categories must be so phrased and defined that any single unit scored cannot fall into more than one category. During scoring, each unit is placed in its appropriate category. After all units are scored, each category is summed and the sums are compared, graphically, by contingency tables, or by some statistical measure. Look carefully at the differences and similarities between and within categories. Reject, or fail to reject, your hypothesis on the basis of what the data comparison shows.

## STUDENT RESEARCH: CONTENT ANALYSIS OF *Time* MAGAZINE COVERS

The following example of research, employing the methodology covered in this chapter, is in the student's own words:

It is my intention in this paper to examine the question of whether the 1960's were significantly more politicized in the United States than the 1950's. Did political issues and political personalities have more salience for the American people in the 1960's? Although most commentators assert this to be so, none offers documentary proof of his opinion. The purpose of this project is to test the validity of the opinion that the 1950's were nonpolitical years in comparison with the 1960's.

In my attempt to provide an answer, I performed a content analysis of the covers of *Time* magazine. The editors of this magazine have claimed that the cover of *Time* reflects the most significant topic of interest to the American people during the week of its issue. In my content analysis, I established several categories for scoring and then scored each week's cover for the years 1951–70.

The basic research design is as shown in Figure 1. A concept, *politicization,* was evaluated by employing the subject on the cover of *Time* as an indicator. This was done for two decades, $T_1$ and $T_2$, and a comparison was made between the two by computing the totals for the decades, the means, and the percentages. (Since I have not studied statistics, no elaborate significance test: were possible.)

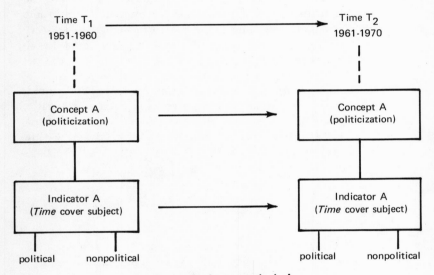

**Figure 1. Basic research design.**

A total of 1,040 covers were scored, 520 per decade; this is the total population of *Time* covers in the years 1951–70.

Major research hypothesis: The decade 1951–60 witnessed lower *political* interest in the United States than the decade 1961–70.

Some minor hypotheses were also tested:

(1) The decade 1951–60 witnessed lower interest in *foreign affairs* in the United States than the decade 1961–70.
(2) The decade 1951–60 witnessed lower interest in *women* in the United States than the decade 1961–70.
(3) The decade 1951–60 witnessed lower interest in *blacks* in the United States than the decade 1961–70.

The last two minor hypotheses were included to measure the extent to which women and blacks obtained recognition and to discover whether these two groups have succeeded in obtaining greater recognition in recent years. The research design is the same for all hypotheses.

All these hypotheses are related to questions regarding the distribution of power and authority in American society and are thus of sociological importance.

## Operationalized Definitions for Establishing Scoring Categories

### POLITICAL

For this project, any cover portraying a person in government or seeking office, or any cover relating to any form of government or policy, was scored as "political." Members of administrations, including cabinet officers or appointees, advisers, and individuals (such as Bobby Baker and Sherman Adams) of political influence were included. Members of the Supreme Court and military leaders were judged on a contextual basis; a biographical sketch of Felix Frankfurter would not be political, while a discussion of the controversy surrounding the Warren Court would be considered political. In some cases, cover stories about nonpolitical individuals might qualify if these people were involved with a political issue then current; for example, Roger Blough during the steel crisis in the Kennedy Administration would qualify. Whenever doubt arose, I read the cover story to determine the cover's content.

### NONPOLITICAL

Any cover not falling in the above category. Thus these two categories are exhaustive and mutually exclusive.

## Categories for Minor Hypotheses

### FOREIGN AFFAIRS

Any cover depicting a foreign country or city was defined as foreign affairs and so scored. Covers showing individuals living outside this country or identified with foreign lands were included. For this project, travel-oriented features were included, as well as any policy related to external affairs.

### DOMESTIC AFFAIRS

Any cover not falling in the above category. Thus these two categories are exhaustive and mutually exclusive.

### WOMEN

Any cover portraying a woman (or biological female, child or adult) or connected with women.

## MEN

Any cover portraying a man (or biological male, child or adult) or connected with men. These categories are not exhaustive, since some covers do not portray individuals but maps and so forth.

## BLACKS

Any cover portraying a black person, American or not.

## NONBLACKS

Any cover portraying a nonblack person, whether Caucasian, Oriental, or Indian. The categories are not exhaustive (see *Men* above).

Each cover was scored once for each of the four hypotheses.

## *Results*

The results of the content analysis of 1,040 covers of *Time* magazine, testing for the salience of the *political* dimension, are shown in Table I. For each year, I have included the number of issues falling into the *political* category; the *nonpolitical* number may be obtained by subtracting the number given from 52 (the number of weeks in a year), since these categories are mutually exclusive and exhaustive.

As these figures indicate, political events and personalities did indeed receive a greater emphasis in the 1960's than in the 1950's. Of the 1960's covers, 58.1 percent were political, but only 51.2 percent of the 1950's covers were so. The average of the ten-year period (*decade mean*) is higher for the 1960's than for the 1950's, and the range is narrower (34 − 26 = 8 but 31 − 18 = 13), showing a smaller dispersion of scores in the 1960's: that is, less "spread" in the number of political covers, year by year, in the 1960's. The 1960's data, therefore, are more homogeneous, since the internal variation is less. Thus I am not able to reject my major hypothesis.

The data reveal some additional characteristics if we group them according to administration, as in Table II. Table II tends to support the contention that the Eisenhower years (1953–60) were relatively nonpolitical. During Eisenhower's second administration (not distinguished in the table), the mean number of political covers was particularly low, 23.75. The inauguration of President Kennedy signaled the beginning

## TABLE I

POLITICAL COVERS OF *Time* MAGAZINE PER YEAR AND DECADE

| Year | T₁ 1951–60 N | Year | T₂ 1961–70 N |
|------|------|------|------|
| 1951 | 31 | 1961 | 29 |
| 1952 | 30* | 1962 | 30 |
| 1953 | 29 | 1963 | 28 |
| 1954 | 26 | 1964 | 32* |
| 1955 | 24 | 1965 | 26 |
| 1956 | 30* | 1966 | 32 |
| 1957 | 24 | 1967 | 31 |
| 1958 | 25 | 1968 | 34* |
| 1959 | 18 | 1969 | 31 |
| 1960 | 28* | 1970 | 29 |

| | |
|---|---|
| Sum = 267 | Sum = 302 |
| Decade mean = 26.7 | Decade mean = 30.2 |
| Range = 18–31 | Range = 26–34 |
| % Political = 51.2% | % Political = 58.1% |
| N = 520 | N = 520 |

\* Election year.

NOTE: The *mean* is the *average* value; add all values to obtain the sum and divide the sum by the number of entries (in this case 10) to obtain the *mean*. The range is the difference between the highest and lowest values obtained in the data set. The *median* is that value above which lie 50 percent of the sample and below which lie the other 50 per cent of the sample. This is often a useful measure, although it has not been employed here.

## TABLE II

DATA REGROUPED TO ACCOUNT FOR PRESIDENTIAL ADMINISTRATION

| Years | Administration | Mean number of political covers |
|------|------|------|
| 1951–52 | Truman | 30.5 |
| 1953–60 | Eisenhower | 25.5 |
| 1961–63 | Kennedy | 29.0 |
| 1964–68 | Johnson | 31.0 |
| 1969–70 | Nixon | 30.0 |

of an era when American life became more politicized, judging by our indicator.

The *foreign affairs* data are shown in Table III. Again, since foreign and domestic affairs are mutually exclusive and exhaustive, the domestic numbers may be obtained by subtracting the yearly numbers given from 52. The results here follow essentially the same pattern as the data on politicization. There is a modest increase in the numbers devoted to foreign affairs in the 1960's. Once again, during the Eisenhower years, especially the second administration, the lowest scores were obtained. Table IV gives these data.

Again, we are unable to reject the hypothesis that the decade 1951–60 witnessed a lower interest in foreign affairs in the United States than the decade 1961–70.

The data on women subjects will not be tabulated separately, since the categories employed are not mutually exclusive and exhaustive. A total of 37 women cover subjects were found for decade $T_1$ and 35 for $T_2$. Hence, women received slightly greater recognition in the 1950's than they did the 1960's on this indicator. Eisenhower's second term represented the nadir of recognition for women, with a mean of only 2; the mean for the Truman years was 5.5, the highest. During the 1950's only 24 American women made the cover, and 14 of these were from

### TABLE III

FOREIGN AFFAIRS COVERS OF *Time* MAGAZINE

| Year | $T_1$ 1951–60 N | Year | $T_2$ 1961–70 N |
|---|---|---|---|
| 1951 | 27 | 1961 | 20 |
| 1952 | 14 | 1962 | 21 |
| 1953 | 21 | 1963 | 23 |
| 1954 | 15 | 1964 | 13 |
| 1955 | 17 | 1965 | 22 |
| 1956 | 17 | 1966 | 19 |
| 1957 | 17 | 1967 | 19 |
| 1958 | 16 | 1968 | 18 |
| 1959 | 10 | 1969 | 19 |
| 1960 | 18 | 1970 | 14 |

| | |
|---|---|
| Sum = 172 | Sum = 188 |
| Decade mean = 17.2 | Decade mean = 18.8 |
| Range = 10–27 | Range = 13–23 |
| % Foreign affairs = 33.1% | % Foreign affairs = 36.1% |

show business, sports, and other entertainment fields. Two of the remaining 10 were related to the incumbent President. One cover was devoted to the "suburban woman."

The situation is similar in the 1960's. Only 22 American women made *Time*'s cover. Of these, 8 were from entertainment fields and 5 were connected with prominent male political

TABLE IV

DATA REGROUPED TO ACCOUNT FOR PRESIDENTIAL ADMINISTRATION

| Years | Administration | Mean number of foreign affairs covers |
|-------|----------------|----------------------------------------|
| 1951–52 | Truman | 20.5 |
| 1953–60 | Eisenhower | 16.3 |
| 1961–63 | Kennedy | 21.3 |
| 1964–68 | Johnson | 18.1 |
| 1969–70 | Nixon | 16.5 |

figures (Martha Mitchell, Marina Oswald, Jackie Kennedy); the remaining 9 included "Mrs. Middle America," the wife in the televised series "An American Family," and a nun portrayed as a symbol of the crisis in the Roman Catholic Church.

During the entire twenty years, only three black women appeared on *Time*'s cover, and all of these came from entertainment fields. We would be inclined to reject our second minor hypothesis, relative to women.

The representation of blacks is slightly worse than that of women. Eleven blacks were represented on *Time* covers in the 1950's, and 18 in the 1960's, accounting for 2.1 percent and 3.5 percent, respectively. This appears to justify the assertion that in America blacks have been ignored more than women. During the 1960's, for all the civil rights activities, of the 18 blacks who made *Time*'s cover only 15 were American, 8 of them from entertainment fields. Three covers depicted issues such as miscegenation and riots. During the 1950's, of the blacks who made the cover, only 5 were American, and these were all from entertainment fields. No black businessman, politician, or community leader was recognized. Thus we cannot reject our hypothesis regarding blacks.

*Conclusions*

*This study has not attempted to evaluate the fidelity with which* Time's *covers do indeed represent the mood and interest of the country.* It has, instead, taken this representation for granted and proceeded to employ the magazine's covers as an indicator of several concepts. Of the four hypotheses, only our second minor hypothesis would be rejected on the basis of these data. No statistical tests were performed, although I understand from another student that I could have tested for differences in means for the two decades on all four sets of categories. But it is not clear to me that this can be done or should be done with a nonrandom sample. Also, this is the complete population of covers, so why test?

The study does sustain the view that the United States was more highly politicized during the 1960's than the 1950's. It also shows that there was more interest in foreign than domestic affairs during the latter decade. Surprisingly, it suggests that women may have been more successful in obtaining recognition in the 1950's than in the 1960's, while blacks received more representation in the 1960's. Both groups, however, were largely ignored by *Time,* and possibly by the American people as well.

The most striking thing about the data is that they do not seem to support the notion that the 1960's constituted a dramatic reversal of the trends of the 1950's. There are differences, but they do not seem to be so great in magnitude as is often claimed.

SUGGESTED READINGS

Amos, Jimmy R., *et al., Statistical Concepts: A Basic Program* (New York: Harper & Row, 1965).

Berelson, Bernard, "Content Analysis," in Gardiner Lindzey (ed.), *Handbook of Social Psychology,* vol. I (Cambridge, Mass.: Addison-Wesley, 1954).

Gerbner, George, and Ole Holsti, *The Analysis of Communication Content* (New York: Wiley, 1968).

Holsti, Ole, *Content Analysis for the Social Sciences and Humanities* (Reading, Mass.: Addison-Wesley, 1969).

Jacobs, Jerry, "A Phenomenological Study of Suicide Notes," *Social Problems* 15, 1967.

Pool, I. deSola, *Trends in Content Analysis* (Urbana: University of Illinois Press, 1959).

Zito, George V., "Durkheimian Suicides in Shakespeare," *Omega* 4, Winter, 1973.

# 3

# *Survey Research*

SURVEY RESEARCH IS A METHODOLOGY *that selects a sample from a larger population in order to discover the interrelations of sociological variables in that population.* It differs from content analysis in that it samples individuals and groups rather than written or published documents. This is done by means of personal interviews, questionnaires, telephone conversations, and panels. Survey research is similar to content analysis in that everything we have noted in Chapter 2 regarding research designs, mutually exclusive and exhaustive categories, concepts, variables, indicators, and contingency tables applies to survey research as well as to content analysis. Thus there are both similarities and differences between the two methodologies.

Since, by the definition given above, inferences or deductions about a larger population are to be made from a smaller sample drawn from that population, it is evident that *the sample must be representative of the population* if the conclusions arrived at are to be valid. This is difficult to accomplish. For one thing, it means that a truly *random* sample must be obtained from the population. In large-scale research, the geographical area from which the sample is to be drawn is first defined, and special statistical measures are employed to select the individuals who are to constitute the sample. Tables of random numbers are available and may be employed in the selection process. Unfortunately, even such measures do not guarantee randomness, because not every person so selected will agree to participate; further, any single sample may overrepresent certain elements of the population. Often a sample is employed that, while not random, is typical in the sense that it includes appropriate *proportional representation* of the various groups the survey is intended to cover. In student research a truly random sample is virtually impossible to obtain, since the sample is usually drawn from people near the researcher's own age, education, and background and is necessarily small in size. Nevertheless, significant student survey research has been done and can be done, provided the findings are restricted to understanding the specific group surveyed.

Although nonparametric statistical measures are applicable to content analysis, survey research generally employs parametric measures; * if the sample is small, however, nonparametric measures are possible. The student whose report on an analysis of the covers of *Time* magazine concluded Chapter 2 quite rightly refrained from employing a parametric test on his nonrandom sample. He probably should not generalize to the larger American population on the basis of his sample and is careful to note in his hypotheses that he is judging by the covers alone. Because he has sampled the entire population of *Time* covers for the years considered, his results are truly representative of *Time* magazine, if not of the nation. Whether the magazine lives up to its claim of reflecting the national mood he leaves unexplored.

Survey-research results are familiar to the student in the form published by the Gallup or Harris poll: "42% for, 30% against, 28% no opinion." In social science, however, we are less interested in what individuals claim to believe than in

---

* In general, parametric measures attempt to determine the characteristics of an entire population (for example, how Americans are distributed with respect to income, religion, occupation, and so forth) on the basis of samples drawn from the population. The relations between the samples and the population are based upon certain mathematical probabilities, and inferences are made to the population on the basis of how random errors occur. Nonparametric measures, on the other hand, do not generalize to the larger population on the basis of randomness but are limited to evaluating the samples themselves and the relationship of properties within them.

determining the conditions under which particular events
are apt to occur. We are interested primarily in activity, not
in superficialities. We are also interested in uncovering the
underlying structures that make society possible and make
change possible.

It is not clear that what a person claims to believe is directly
related to what he does. It makes little sense to furnish people
with a questionnaire and then take the answers they supply
at face value, although some social scientists do precisely this.
In many instances, the replies furnished are normative responses:
they are the replies the respondent feels he ought to give or
believes the questioner expects him to give. They are *not* "true."
It is not that the respondent is consciously lying to the questioner; it is simply that, of the possible options offered to him,
only certain ones are admissible to strangers according to the
prevailing *norms* of his sociocultural group. If what you wish
to determine in your research *are* the norms of the respondent's
group, then such a procedure may be acceptable. But if the
target of your research is not these norms but factual behavior,
then you must somehow control for normative responses.

There is a marked difference between what Max Weber called
the existential and the normative, and these must not be
confused. The *normative* is what is prescribed, what one feels
"ought" to be done; it is a product of one's social conditioning,
or socialization. The *factual* is what actually occurs in human
behavior, no matter what logic, custom, and professed morals
dictate. Very few persons in our society will openly oppose peace,
love, and universal brotherhood, for example; but their actual
behavior in very few cases will be in accordance with these
values. These attitudes and sentiments have been prescribed
for thousands of years, but the history of those years is one of
continual war, bloodshed, and indifference, not one of love,
peace, and brotherhood.

From what has been said thus far, it is apparent that survey
research has probably been employed more often than it should
be. According to the definition given on page 56, survey research
is a methodolgy that seeks to discover the interrelations among
sociological variables. These should be *significant* variables,
capable of yielding substantive meaning in terms of social

theory. Yet survey research has most frequently dealt with the trivial or obvious. Moreover, survey responses have often been taken as literally true, particularly in political science. The success of surveys in market research and advertising is due less to any merit of this technique than to interpretations by the Madison Avenue entrepreneurs who abuse it.

## TYPES OF SURVEY

Telephone and mail "questionnaires" are of little use in responsible survey research; their results are open to question, and the poor returns usually introduce insurmountable problems in interpretation. There is virtually no way to obtain a sample that is representative of the population to be studied. If the survey involves a very large sample, then a large number of trained interviewers will be needed. This requires money, time, and patience. For these reasons, surveys by telephone or mail should be avoided.

If a survey is worth conducting at all, it is worth conducting in person, via face-to-face interviews. Student-conducted research should be limited to small samples. It is this very aspect of the methodology that makes student-conducted research at least as good as many of the large, nationwide surveys. In the latter, it is virtually impossible to obtain the degree of control necessary to render the results meaningful.

There are two distinct types of interviews. One employs a survey *instrument* (or *schedule*), often in the form of a questionnaire. The interviewer reads the questions to the respondent, one at a time, and records his responses. Sometimes the entire schedule is handed to the respondent and he completes it himself. Of these alternatives, the first is preferable. It enables the respondent to ask questions about the wording and meaning or intention of the question posed. Most important, it involves the researcher and the respondent in a social situation that is less contrived and artificial than the second alternative. For the respondent, filling out a questionnaire on his own is very much like taking an examination: He tries to guess the "correct" answers, or tries to find a pattern in the questions.

Of course, the very nature of the survey may require the

respondent to fill in the answers himself, particularly if the instrument employs graphic forms or figures. But even with this variety it is advisable for the researcher to discuss the figures or scales informally with the respondent as the latter completes the schedule. This not only helps the researcher to develop interactional proficiency for his future researches but enables him to spot and thereafter improve questions of dubious wording or conceptual difficulty. Indeed, before attempting to employ a survey instrument that one has devised, it is always necessary to make several "dry runs" with it on friends and associates, to *pretest* the adequacy of the questions it contains. Those items presenting unusual difficulty for respondents should be reworked for maximal clarity.

The second type of interview is the *open-ended interview*. In such an interview a schedule, as such, is not usually employed. Instead, the researcher commits to memory the essential categories of his research design and, in a normal, conversational manner, encourages the respondent to speak about each of these in turn. The exact phrasing of the interviewer's questions should be in the form most natural to him in his ordinary conversations. He may make coded notes of the respondent's answers as they occur or, better still, record the entire interview on tape to be coded later. Coding here takes the identical form it does in content analysis; indeed, *the open-ended interview is essentially a content-analysis technique combined with an interview.* It has the best features of both methods and can therefore provide the greatest yield of *meaning,* which is what we are seeking. The researcher listens for the occurrence of certain preselected categories, previously defined in his research design, and codes them as described in Chapter 2. Open-ended interviews involve nothing less than the content analysis of oral, rather than written, communications. Moreover, they train the researcher to listen carefully. It is suprising how much information is lost in normal conversation as a result of short-term lapses of attention on the part of participants. Learning to listen can be as important for the social researcher as learning to see subtle color variations is for the painter.

Of the two types of interview, my own preference is for the open-ended, for it imposes fewer artificial constraints on the respondents. People soon forget the tape recorder; they are not distracted by mysterious note-taking on the part of the interviewer; generally, once they begin talking, the only problem the researcher faces is how to turn them off one question and on to the next. It is a natural and informal type of interview, producing the least strain between participants.

It almost goes without saying that whenever possible the interview should be conducted on the respondent's terrain rather than the researcher's. If the research is related to occupational variables, it should be conducted where the respondent works. Terrain is dictated by the nature of the research problem, not by the convenience of the parties to the interview. The respondent should be in a position to assume the *social role* appropriate to the specific research problem. This means, for example, that if the research is concerned with the problems of students, the interviews must be conducted on campus. People are not students off campus, since that role is not prescribed except on campus. No one is a student during vacation or semester breaks; the interactional situations one encounters on those occasions are seldom such that one is coerced into assuming the student role. Even a policeman is not really a policeman off duty, when he is mending his socks or performing any other tasks not related to his job. Individuals are called upon to perform many social roles. It is necessary, in conducting social research, to know whether one is interviewing a policeman or a sock-mender, and the only way to ensure this is to conduct the interview under conditions in which the prescribed role must be performed.

The *panel survey* is a method employing a select group, who comprise a *panel*. The literature describes two distinct kinds of panel surveys. In one type, selected experts or specialists presumed to be knowledgeable on the question being investigated are asked to rank or rate a series of items, and the researcher then determines the degree of agreement on the basis of the results. In the second type, the same group is surveyed more than once. This enables the researcher to check his original results at a later time by employing the same people. He may be interested in testing the persistence of an attitude or in introducing some new item and determining its effect by a "before and after" experiment. Panel surveys will not be covered in this book.

SCHEDULE DESIGN

The design of a high-quality research schedule is complex; the most we can do here is to introduce the basic requirements and provide sufficient information for the student to get under way. For the past twenty years, survey research has been the most widely employed of all research methods, and many excellent texts are available.* The serious student should consult current issues of the sociology journals (the *American Sociological Review* and the *American Journal of Sociology*) for examples of professional work in this method.

Whether the schedule is filled out by the respondent or interviewer, and whether or not an open-ended interview is conducted, a *cover sheet* is necessary for demographic information. This page includes a space for the respondent's name or identifying number, his address, age, sex, marital status, race or ethnic identity, level of education, income, number of children, and whatever other demographic data are of possible relevance to the research. The respondent must be assured of the confidentiality of this information and must feel free to decline to give certain information if he so chooses. Other information requested is determined largely by the nature of the research problem. A number should be assigned to each respondent's completed schedule, and in data analysis he should be known to the researcher only by number. The identity of respondents *must* be kept confidential, and information given by them must not be disclosed under any circumstances to *anyone*. Some researchers do not include a space for the respondent's name on the cover sheet but only a number; the name associated with that number can be filed separately so that the researcher is not tempted to make the identification but can always recheck his sources, if necessary, by consulting the file.

If the schedule is of the questionnaire variety, the questions to be asked depend entirely on the research design. As with content analysis—or any other technique, for that matter—the design must be thought through before any attempt is made to use it

---

* See, for example, William B. Sanders, *The Sociologist as Detective: An Introduction to Research Methods* (New York: Praeger, 1974), and James A. Davis, *Elementary Survey Analysis* (Englewood Cliffs, N.J.: Prentice-Hall, 1971).

as the basis of an instrument for measurement. This means writing down the concepts and indicators and the basic relationships in the form of hypotheses and considering the possible results that may occur in the form of contingency tables. Unless this can be done and adequately diagrammed, it is doubtful that the research can actually be performed. It is best to work out the design in the form of diagrams similar to those of Figures 2–2 through 2–6, before attempting to phrase any questions.

The actual form of the questions is dictated by the kind of analysis one intends to perform, and this is in turn dictated by the kinds of scales used for indicators. It may be that a scale is not being employed, that one is simply counting the number of persons responding favorably to a single question and the number who respond unfavorably and then comparing the results. Although this sounds almost too simple, it is suggested as a good way to start. Suppose, for example, that one is testing the hypothesis that socialization processes in the form of peer-group pressures are more effective with freshmen than with seniors. In its most elementary form, this research may involve nothing more than standing on campus, stopping every third person, and asking whether he or she is either a freshman or a senior. Those who give a positive reply might then be asked a question regarding their attitude toward some current problem or an "in" fashion of the time. One records the fact that so many freshmen agree with the "in" fashion, so many do not, and the same information for the seniors. The only demographic datum obtained in this example is the school year of the respondents, which can be treated conceptually as constituting the independent variable (X). The dependent variable (Y) is the attitude toward the "in" fashion. Note that we are not actually revealing our hypothesis to the respondents. They are most likely to assume that what we are really trying to learn is whether they are "with it" or not. We might finally arrive at the results shown in Figure 3–1. Here a sample of 28 freshmen and 32 seniors was questioned, with the results shown. Remember that each cell contains the number of respondents who fall into two categories, one each on the X and Y variables.

Although we could not, on the basis of such a simple survey, generalize our results to a population beyond our campus, they do reveal differences between the freshmen and the seniors we

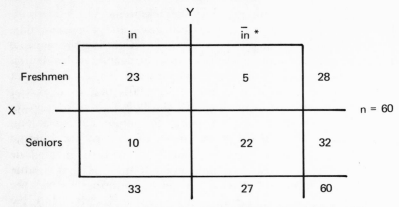

**Figure 3-1. A four-celled contingency table showing a positive relationship between X and Y.**

*Read $\overline{\text{in}}$ as "not in." The stroke above "in" means *not,* or the negation of what is beneath it.

have interviewed, differences that we might suspect contain a measure of validity. Of course, we are not sure that the distribution shown in Figure 3–1 is the result of a condition in which Y is really dependent on X, in the form

It could conceivably be of the form

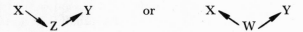

In the XZY case, Z is known as an *intervening variable.* It may be, for example, that on this campus freshmen are confined to dorms, while seniors are not; Z, here, could be *dormitory confinement.* Hence, one reason we obtain the results of Figure 3–1 might be not that peer-group pressures are more effective with freshmen but that seniors living off campus spend less time in the presence of their peers and hence are not subjected to the same intensity of peer pressures as are the freshmen. In other words, the effectiveness of peer-group pressures may not be involved in the differences we find.

To *control* for this possibility, we could have asked one more bit of information from our respondents: whether they live on campus or off. Then we could separate, in our contingency table, those living in dorms and those who do not and look at the differences between seniors and freshmen falling into these two groups. We might obtain the results shown in Figure 3–2.

| Z | | Y in | Y $\overline{in}$ | |
|---|---|---|---|---|
| Dormitory residence | freshmen | 20 | 4 | 24 |
| | seniors | 9 | 2 | 11 |
| Off-campus residence | freshmen | 3 | 1 | 4 |
| | seniors | 1 | 20 | 21 |
| | | 33 | 27 | 60 |

X — n = 60

**Figure 3-2. The effect of the intervening variable Z, place of residence, in the XY relationship of Figure 3-1.**

Figure 3–2 has been constructed in such a way that we can *control* for the possible effect of the intervening variable Z, *place of residence*. The same 28 freshmen and 32 seniors as in Figure 3–1 have been tabulated, this time taking place of residence into account.* Of the 11 seniors living in dorms, 9 are favorably inclined to the "in" fashion; of the 24 freshmen in dorms, 20 are favorably inclined. The few freshmen not living in dorms probably commute. The results of Figure 3–2 may show how new fads diffuse through a student community, but they do *not* justify the assumption that peer-group socialization is more effective with freshmen than seniors. The research has not been wasted, however, for it suggests other research we might conduct, such as an exploration of how such diffusion takes place in small groups.

---

* It is important to look at the right-hand marginals. Note that 24 freshmen live in dorms, and 4 live off campus; thus $24 + 4 = 28$. Dorm seniors $= 11$, off campus $= 21$; thus $11 + 21 = 32$.

Let's consider the case in which a *spurious relationship* occurs. A variable W may cause both X and Y to vary together; in such a case, the variation in Y is not a result of any variation in X, although if we did not know about the existence of W we might believe that X affected Y directly.* Suppose that W is the variable *geographical origin* of the student. The freshman class may all have come from the same state owing to the college's recruitment practices. Since the dropout rate is high for freshmen and sophomores, there is a likelihood that upperclassmen include many transfers from out-of-state colleges while lowerclassmen are mainly local students. In other words, the freshman class is more *homogeneous* with respect to origin than the senior class and hence contains less *variation* within it. Since fads and fashions can be expected to be dispersed on an area basis, it is not surprising to obtain the results of Figure 3–1.

If it is true that geographical origin explains most of the variation found in the dependent variable Y, we should be able to determine this by controlling for geographical origin of the students, just as we previously controlled for place of residence. This means that during the interview we must ask the respondents an additional question regarding state of origin; we now need three pieces of demographic data, not simply one, as in our original example. This shows the importance of thinking through one's research design before attempting to collect data; the possible contingencies must be evaluated prior to questionnaire design in order to determine what questions must be asked. If we do not do this, we have no way to control for possibilities associated with other hypotheses than our own; and while the results we obtain may appear to bolster our assumption regarding the relationship between X and Y, they may not in fact do so.

If we had asked for state of origin and school year but not for residence, we might obtain results such as those of Figure 3–3. These results show about the same number of out-of-state and

---

* For an interesting discussion of such relationships at the elementary level, see Stephen Cole, *The Sociological Method* (Chicago: Markham, 1972). This inexpensive text is a good introduction to survey analysis. The title is misleading, however. Survey analysis is not *the* sociological method, as I have attempted to show in the previous chapters, but only one of many sociological methods, no one of which can claim priority over the others.

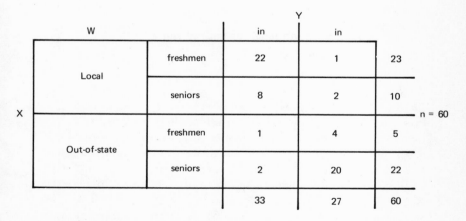

| W | | Y in | Y $\overline{\text{in}}$ | |
|---|---|---|---|---|
| Local | freshmen | 11 | 3 | 14 |
| | seniors | 4 | 12 | 16 |
| Out-of-state | freshmen | 12 | 2 | 14 |
| | seniors | 6 | 10 | 16 |
| | | 33 | 27 | 60 |

X — n = 60

Figure 3-3. The absence of effect of variable W, place of origin, on the XY relationship of Figure 3-1.

local students in each category of the dependent variable. Hence, W does not seem to have much effect. Had we obtained the results shown in Figure 3–4, however, we would be forced to conclude that any relationship between X and Y disclosed by

| W | | Y in | Y in | |
|---|---|---|---|---|
| Local | freshmen | 22 | 1 | 23 |
| | seniors | 8 | 2 | 10 |
| Out-of-state | freshmen | 1 | 4 | 5 |
| | seniors | 2 | 20 | 22 |
| | | 33 | 27 | 60 |

X — n = 60

Figure 3-4. The effect of variable W on the relationship of X and Y of Figure 3-1, demonstrating that the XY relationship is a spurious one.

| W | Z | X | Y in | Y $\overline{in}$ | |
|---|---|---|---|---|---|
| Local | dormitory residence | freshmen | 20 | 0 | 20 |
| | | seniors | 8 | 2 | 10 |
| | off-campus residence | freshmen | 2 | 1 | 3 |
| | | seniors | 0 | 0 | 0 |
| Out-of-state | dormitory residence | freshmen | 1 | 0 | 1 |
| | | seniors | 1 | 0 | 1 |
| | off-campus residence | freshmen | 0 | 4 | 4 |
| | | seniors | 1 | 20 | 21 |
| n = 60 | | | 33 | 27 | 60 |

Figure 3-5. Controlling for both W and Z in the XY relationship of Figure 3-1.

these data is a spurious one, for here W, geographical origin, does indeed explain most, but not all, of the variation in Y.

Figure 3–5 shows the possible results if we had asked for geographical origin, year, *and* residence. These three pieces of information yield a 16-cell contingency table, for we are controlling for W and Z and looking at the relationship between X and Y. Thus four variables are involved. In this figure we see some of the effects of employing so small a sample. Empty cells are beginning to appear, and the number of respondents falling into any one cell is small. Obviously, if we break our sample into 16 rather than 4 or 8 parts, each part stands a good chance of being smaller than before. (We will have more to say concerning this possibility in a later chapter, for it has implications of a more theoretical nature that we can not discuss at this point.)

If we found that geographical origin did not explain much of the variation in our results, as in Figure 3–3, we would not be in any particular difficulty. As a matter of fact, we would be better off, for we could assert that, on the basis of our results, geographical origin was insignificant. In similar fashion we could control for any number of variables that *might* affect our results and, by constructing the appropriate contingency table for each variable's effect upon Y with X included, decide how much variation, if any, is explained by each variable.

What we have considered thus far should clarify the need for completeness in the cover sheet of the schedule and the whole idea of controlling for variations in the dependent variable. Most important, we not only explain the effects we uncover but find ourselves understanding how groups and societies are constituted and how differentiated they really are.

The operation of controlling for effects, discussed above, is an excellent example of the basic analytical process of comparing categories. It enables us to explain the variation we find in our dependent variable. Whether or not one intends to do survey research, the fundamentals discussed in this chapter are essential to any sociological analysis employing any methodology. Similarly, the idea of *explained variation,* to which this is related, finds widespread application in a variety of methods. We can, if we so choose, express the percentage explained variation resulting from any of our controlling operations and thereby show the relative degree to which many independent variables contribute to an effect found in a dependent variable.*

In our preceding examples, we have used a single dichotomous variable as the dependent variable, "in" and "īn." I purposely did not specify any "in" fashion, not only because fads come and go so quickly, but also because I wished to encourage the

---

* Students with quantitative aptitudes might consider how the marginals of Figure 3–5 might be converted into percentages. What percentage of the difference between in and īn is explained by geographical origin? By place of residence?

student to think in terms of categories rather than distract him by some specific item. The method, after all, is one of categories, not specifics, and it is methodology that we are discussing. The student should have no difficulty supplying specific examples.

As in our example in discussing content analysis, we dichotomized our dependent variable Y into a plus and a minus, in/in, yes/no, a two-valued scale. The dependent variable can be any property, effect, activity, or attribute. It may be elicited by questions of the "do you or don't you" variety ("Do you approve of legislation to legalize dope?" "Do you think abortion laws should be outlawed?") or of the variety calling for a numerical response, such as "How many times a week would you say you do such and such?" In the latter case, the "how many times" can be dichotomized, scoring plus for any response that states a number greater than zero and minus for any negative response, such as "not at all," "never," and so on. In other words, any response showing that the respondent engages in the activity, no matter what the frequency, could be scored as a "yes." What we are interested in when we employ dichotomous variables is the presence or absence of an activity or property, not its intensity. In the examples given, the *unit of anaylsis* is the *person*, and the table cells show the frequency with which persons fall into these categories. Hence, each cell contains a number of persons, *not* the scores obtained by the persons. This is a critical distinction and must be kept in mind. Note that, true to our argument in Chapter 2, we have kept categories not only mutually exclusive (no unit of analysis can fall into more than one cell) but exhaustive as well, since *our hypothesis was phrased concerning only seniors and freshmen.* The categories need not exhaust every possibility in the universe, but *only those possibilities involved in the hypothesis,* which defines the specific universe considered.

Suppose that we wished to determine whether freshmen or seniors experienced more alienation. Alienation is a complex concept. As a sociological construct, it has been operationalized by Melvin Seeman and others. In performing on-campus or dormitory research, we may be interested in the intensity of alienation in these two groups, perhaps as a result of a research design that predicts higher alienation among freshmen than seniors. Such a prediction may come about as a result of a belief that freshmen, who are less *integrated* into the academic community than are seniors, are more likely to experience *powerlessness, normlessness,* and *social estrangement* than are seniors. These are three dimensions of alienation that Seeman found occurring frequently in the alienation literature.* We expect that high integration within a community will result in lower feelings of alienation within that community.

Since alienation is central to much social theory and plays a leading part in the work of Marx, Durkheim, Merton, and others, it is a theoretically significant variable, worth considering in research projects. The concepts of *powerlessness, normlessness,* and *social isolation* are of a lower order of abstraction than *alienation* and therefore may be measurable.

Unlike our previous examples in this section, the dependent variable here is one that may not be easily dichotomized. Since this concept is reducible to three separate dimensions, each dimension should be measured on each unit of analysis. But the problem is even greater than this, for one cannot assess whether the respondent experiences, let us say, *normlessness* on the basis of a single answer to a single question. A series of questions must be asked for *each* dimension. A *multiple index score* is then obtained for each respondent, and the scores of freshmen are compared with the scores of seniors.

To keep matters manageable, let us suppose that we are going to ask three questions for each of the three dimensions, or a total of nine questions in our questionnaire. We need to have operationalized definitions of our three concepts before we can phrase questions that might serve as indicators.

*Powerlessness* has been operationalized as the expectancy held by the individual that his or her behavior cannot determine the outcomes he or she seeks.

*Normlessness* has been operationalized as the expectancy that socially disapproved behaviors are required to achieve desired goals.

*Social isolation* (or *social estrangement*) has been operationalized as the assignment of low reward value to goals or beliefs highly valued in the society or group.

What we must do is phrase three questions for each of these

---

* Seeman also found evidence of *isolation, meaninglessness,* and *self-estrangement,* but these will not be considered here.

operationalizations and use these questions as indicators of the presence or absence of that aspect of alienation in the respondents. Each respondent will then be given an alienation *score*. Bear in mind that the questions must be phrased according to the population to be sampled. That is, since we are hypothesizing about a student population, the questions should reflect a student orientation or concern. The completed schedule may take the following form:

1. Do you feel that you personally can do anything to improve the conditions on campus that everyone is objecting to?
2. It has been suggested that a group of students meet with the administration to clarify the current ruling on pets in dorms. Would you be willing to serve on such a committee?
3. Do you feel it would help if students wrote to their state legislators complaining about conditions on this campus?
4. Some students suggest that conditions here can be improved only if we do something illegal. Do you agree with this?
5. Do you feel that in a school like this one *must* cheat on exams to get by?
6. Do you often find yourself doing what you know is not acceptable to others on campus?
7. Most students here seem to think highly of the new chancellor. What do you think of him?
8. There are so many activities here that it's difficult to keep up with them. and most people seem to like them. How often do you attend these activities?
9. Most students here are opposed to the university's conducting government-sponsored research of a military nature. How do you feel about it?

Questions 1 through 3 are intended to evaluate the dimension of *powerlessness*, 4 through 6 that of *normlessness*, and 7 through 9 that of *social estrangement*. Compare these with the operationalized definitions. Note, too, that the respondent probably would think that we were conducting the survey in order to evaluate the school rather than anything so abstract as student alienation. The exact wording, including the issues involved, is suited to a particular campus context; other wordings may be more suitable for other campuses. A "no" answer or its equivalent on one of the first three questions is scored +1, but a "yes" is not scored. (Remember that the *higher* the score, the *greater* the alienation.) The next three questions, 4 through 6, have been so phrased that a "yes" response yields a score of one for each while "no" is not scored, reversing the previous approach to scoring. This is to minimize what is known as *response set,* or the tendency on the part of the respondent to answer all questions in the same way without really thinking about what he is doing. It is a good practice in the construction of any schedule to make provisions for doing this. One may also insert questions completely unrelated to the research problem to minimize the respondent's ability to predict the problem under consideration. Sometimes the same question may be asked twice, but in a disguised form, to check the attentiveness of the respondent; this is particularly important if the respondent is filling out the questionnaire himself rather than answering an interviewer's questions. Question 7 is scored 1 if the respondent does not think highly of the chancellor; Question 8 is scored 1 if the respondent replies that he or she does not attend frequently; Question 9 is scored 1 if the respondent does not share the popular view.

Each respondent can thus attain an alienation score ranging from 0 to 9. Since we are *weighting* each dimension equally—that is, since we are assuming that each dimension is as representative of alienation as the other two—a score of 0–4 can be characterized as "low alienation," while one from 5–9 can be characterized as "high alienation." * If we dichotomize the resulting scores in this way, we are losing a certain amount of information, but once again we may construct a straightforward four-celled contingency table and see whether the relationship holds. We might obtain the results shown in Figure 3–6. The figure shows that the predicted relationship is found; seniors are less alienated than freshman. On the basis of the information on our cover sheet, we could go through operations of control similar to those we performed in evaluating the "in" relationship. Is alienation stronger among those living in dorms or off campus? Is it a function of place of origin? How much of the variation is explained by these variables? By such controls, we may learn much more than we had expected. How important is the sex of the respondent in determining alienation? Are

* We refer to the value at which we divide the scores into two parts as the "cutting point." In this example, the cutting point has been established between 4 and 5.

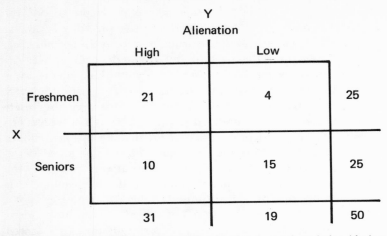

Figure 3-6. A four-celled contingency table showing a *negative* relationship between student educational level and degree of experienced alienation. Note the high level of alienation for both seniors and freshmen, however. Read the cell headings carefully.

females more alienated than males, or vice versa? What, if anything, does this tell us about the degree of integration of female students on this campus? Since our primary concern is with integration, what have we learned about integration processes in a student society?

It may be, of course, that we find no significant differences between the two groups in levels of alienation when we control for sex, school year, and the like. In fact, the marginals of Figure 3–6 disclose only a weak relationship, for high levels of alienation are experienced by 31 of the 50 cases. Whether we reject or fail to reject our hypothesis depends on the degree of difference found in the diagorrals.

SCALES

In attempting to measure alienation, we treated each of the three dimensions as carrying equal weight. Suppose a respondent scored 3 on questions 1 through 3 and 0 on the others. This would mean that his score was a result of the operationalization of the category *powerlessness*. If another respondent with a score of 3 scored 0 on questions 1 through 3 as well as on questions 7 through 9, this would mean that his score was a result of the operationalization of the category *normlessness*. Similarly, a third may have scored 3 only on questions 7 through 9, indicating *social estrangement*. Since each of these cases has a score of 3, we had to place it in the *low alienation* category. But is this conceptually and logically correct?

It may be that a very high degree of social estrangement is required for a respondent to experience as much alienation as he does under a condition of relatively low normlessness or powerlessness. In other words, it may be that we should weight normlessness and powerlessness higher than social estrangement —for example, requiring a score of, say, 2 in social estrangement to equal a score of 1 in powerlessness or normlessness. We could accomplish this by providing six questions instead of three in the social-estrangement category and scoring each ½ point instead of 1. This allows us to keep our cutting point between *high* and *low* about where it was and a possible total alienation score of 9, as we had. Thus, instead of 0–4 being considered low, we would now consider 0–4.5 as low and anything above it as high. But do we really have any right to weight these variables this way, without some proof that social estrangement is indeed only half as effective as either of the other two? We do not, and therefore we should not. We may weight variables only when there is sufficient evidence that they *must* be weighted. To do otherwise is to stack the cards in our own favor by predicting a relationship and then deciding which way the various parts of the scores are to be considered.

In addition, there is no real way of knowing whether each of these questions has the same weight; nevertheless, we simply added the totals as if they did. That is certainly not the best methodological procedure.

These kinds of considerations have led methodologists to consider the construction of scales to measure the intensity of a variable. One of the earliest such scales was the so-called Thurstone scale, which has since fallen into disuse. The Thurstone scale is constructed by employing a version of the panel survey discussed earlier in this chapter. A panel of "experts" is asked to rank a series of items, which apparently reflect varying intensities of a concept, and the most frequent ranking is taken as consensual validation of that ranking. Thus, if most "experts" agree that normlessness represents a lower intensity of alienation than powerlessness, and social estrangement the lowest intensity, then powerlessness might be given a value of 3, normlessness a value of 2, and social estrangement a value of 1. Although the Thurstone method of scaling was very popular in the 1930's, it has since become discredited. For one thing, it proved time-consuming and required too many judges or "experts." It does not eliminate the principal problem, that the same sum can indicate many different patterns of response. Moreover, it often appeared that the assigned values were influenced more by one's choice of "experts" than by any property of the concept itself!

To overcome some of these disadvantages, the Likert scaling method was introduced. With Likert scales, the respondent is required to check one point on a graded scale for each question, either orally (to the interviewer) or on the schedule itself. For example, Question 1 of our alienation schedule could be reworked in the following form:

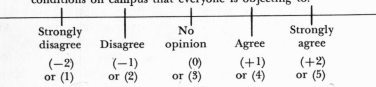

The individual student can do nothing to improve the conditions on campus that everyone is objecting to.

| Strongly disagree | Disagree | No opinion | Agree | Strongly agree |
|---|---|---|---|---|
| (−2) or (1) | (−1) or (2) | (0) or (3) | (+1) or (4) | (+2) or (5) |

Here the respondent must encircle one choice (or have it encircled for him by the interviewer). The scale shown above is a 5-point Likert scale; if the researcher wishes finer gradations, it could be expanded to a 7-point scale by inserting *mildly disagree* between *no opinion* and *disagree* and *mildly agree* between *no opinion* and *agree*. The values assigned are shown in parentheses, but these should not appear on the schedule if the respondent is to encircle the answers himself. Note that the higher the score, the greater the powerlessness perceived.

The Likert scale is an *ordinal scale:* Although the values are in rank order or progress arithmetically, they may not be divided or multiplied together because the space between units may not be equal in intensity. That each unit, however, is higher than the preceding unit, commencing at −2 and progressing to +2, seems apparent. Likert scales are easy to construct, they have a high retest reliability, and the choice of intensity is determined by the respondent rather than a panel of "experts." They also lend themselves to more advanced quantitative-analysis techniques. The student should attempt to construct similar scales for the other items of the alienation schedule by rephrasing the questions. Likert scales are highly recommended to the student for his own survey research efforts.

If many such scales are employed in a single schedule, a *halo effect* may develop in the respondent as a *response set;* that is, he may find himself automatically checking the same intensity point on each item. As mentioned previously, this tendency may be minimized by phrasing the question or statement in such a way that the polarity is reversed occasionally, by inserting *filler items* or dummy scales that are left out of the final tabulation, and by randomly arranging the items so that not all of those measuring the same property follow each other on the page. Unfortunately, the Likert scale method does *not* correct for different response patterns yielding the same score.

The scale divisions need not be of the *agree/disagree* form; *strong/weak* or any other measure of intensity may be employed. It is important, however, to phrase the statement preceding the scale so that it expresses an extreme positive or negative polarity in its intention. Thus "The individual can do *nothing*" is required, *not* "The individual can't do *very much.*"

Before leaving scaling methods, two other scales must be mentioned. The first of these is the Guttman scale. This scale has a *cumulative* or *transitive* property, since each interval includes those preceding it.

Earlier in this section we discussed the possibility of weighting variables in order to account for possible differences in their significance in determining outcomes. It was mentioned that variables may be weighted only when there is sufficient evidence that they *must* be. Giving one item more importance than another item is possible only if the concept under evaluation is truly *unidimensional.* Unidimensionality cannot be assumed; it must be demonstrated. The concept *alienation* was shown to be *multidimensional,* composed of at least two or more dimensions, such as normlessness, powerlessness, and so on. If, however, we knew that individuals experienced social estrangement *before* they experienced normlessness, and experienced normlessness *before* they were able to experience powerlessness, this would point to the possibility that such dimensions as normlessness, powerlessness, and so on were only components of a single dimension. If these dimensions could be ordered in this way, the concept *alienation* would have to be considered as *unidimensional*. Unfortunately, this is not the case, and we are left with it as a multidimensional form.

Some sociological concepts and constructs do have unidimensional forms. Indeed, a great deal of research is conducted to ascertain such unidimensionality. The Guttman scaling procedure is one technique that has been developed for determining unidimensionality. An excellent discussion of Guttman scaling is provided by Matilda White Riley.*

Suppose we were interested in drug use and had determined that some of our respondents used heroin, some marijuana, some hashish, some two of these three, some all three, and so forth. The question might arise whether anyone used heroin who had not smoked marijuana, or anyone used LSD who had not used heroin, and so forth.

Suppose, for the sake of simplicity, that we confine our analysis to heroin and marijuana. We could construct a four-celled table such as that of Figure 3–7a, in which we tallied the respondents by drug use, using (+) for use and (−) for nonuse. Let's look at this table in a somewhat different way from previous contingency tables. For the moment, let's not put units of analysis into the cells. Instead, let's simply identify the cells by placing within them the plus or minus of each margin: In other words, the first row of two cells gets a plus in each of the two cells from heroin, while the second row gets a minus in each of the two cells from pot; the first column gets a plus for pot in each cell, but a minus for pot is given to each cell of column 2, as shown in Figure 3–7b. Since we are attempting to measure the degree of drug use, it is apparent that respondents who should fall into the cell containing (−−) represent minimal drug use, while those falling into the cell containing (++)

* Matilda White Riley, *Sociological Research: A Case Approach* (New York: Harcourt, Brace & World, 1963). See chap. 9, from which this example is drawn.

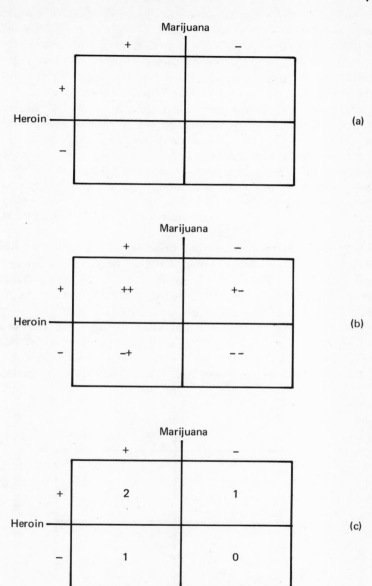

Figure 3-7. Steps in the evolution of a Guttman scale of drug use.

represent our maximal drug use for these two drugs. If we were to score a 0 for a negative (−) and a 1 for a (+), we would have the table shown in Figure 3–7c.

This figure suggests a possible scale of drug use ranging in value from 0 to 2. We might rate our respondents on a scale from 0 to 2, depending upon which drugs they use. But is this logical? Cells (+−) and (−+) each yield a score of 1. But the user of cell (+−) employs heroin and not marijuana, and the user of cell (−+) employs marijuana and not heroin. We know that heroin is an addictive drug for most users, but evidence shows that marijuana is not, although both are drugs by law. We might suspect that anyone who uses heroin might not think twice about using marijuana, but that users of marijuana might indeed think twice before attempting to use heroin. On the basis of this reasoning, we might doubt that the (+−) cell condition represents something possible, or at least conclude that it is a highly *unlikely* possibility; in other words, this cell stands a high probability of turning up empty. Few, if any, units of analysis should fall into this cell. We can collect our data and then assign each unit of analysis to the appropriate cell. If we did this and found that what we suspected was borne out by our results—that cell (+−) was essentially empty and most of our cases fell into the other three cells—then we would drop cell (+−), disclosing the pattern of Figure 3–8. Since the

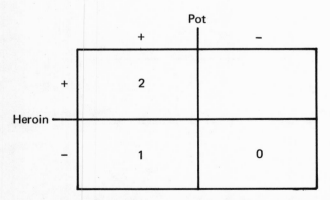

Figure 3-8. Elimination of a null cell, resulting in a three-value scale for drug use.

(+ −) cell has been eliminated, this suggests a three-value scale ranging from 0 to 2, where the score obtained by the respondent has a unique value and is unambiguous. There is only one possible way to obtain a score on this scale. Figure 3–9 restates the meaning of Figure 3–8 for each score. Notice that the scale shows that the respondents who use no drugs obtain a score of 0, those who use only marijuana a score of 1, and those who use both a score of 2. Notice further that if a respondent gets a score of 2, it means that he uses not only marijuana but heroin as well, and that *to use heroin means that one also uses marijuana.*

| Score on scale | Heroin | Marijuana |
|:--------------:|:------:|:---------:|
| 2 | + | + |
| 1 | − | + |
| 0 | − | − |

Figure 3–9.  A Guttman scale of drug use.

The scale is *cumulative,* or progressive: Score 2 is greater than score 1, and score 1 is greater than 0—in meaning, not just in number. If the data do arrange themselves in such a manner that the construction of a Guttman scale is possible, then the *unidimensional* nature of the variable (i.e., *drug use*) is determined. Most important, unlike Likert scaling, the scale of Figure 3–9 does not yield the same score for two different response patterns.

By such procedures as these, an entire Guttman scale may be constructed, ranging from amphetamines and barbiturates through the hallucinogens and hard drugs. Once such a scale has been obtained, the researcher knows that if a respondent has taken a particular drug, there is a high probability of his having used the drugs beneath it on the Guttman scale of drug use. Guttman scales are, however, relatively difficult to construct. A coefficient may be constructed, ranging from 0 to 1 and designated as R, which tells us how predictive the scale is. This coefficient must be at least equal to .9 to make sense.

Because of the difficulty encountered in their construction, Guttman scales *per se* are not recommended to the beginning student researcher. Nevertheless, the basic principle of the Guttman scale should be kept in mind in analyzing data. For example, in tabulating results employing contingency tables, the appearance of relatively few (or no) cases in cell (+−) should lead the researcher to consider whether a cumulative property is present that might lead to the possibility that the concept he is measuring is unidimensional. This leads to questioning the equivalence of the (+−) and (−+) categories. If one of these categories can be eliminated, the data may Guttman-scale. If they do, the researcher has made a significant finding about his research problem. The coefficient of reproducibility should be computed, and if it is near .9 or better, the final report should include a statement to this effect.

In Chapter 2, I mentioned the *semantic-differential* scaling technique developed by Charles Osgood and his colleagues.* This technique has been used to measure word concepts and has disclosed that these contain three major dimensions: *potency, evaluative,* and *activity;* that is, strength or intensity, positive or negative estimation, and active/passive. Without an extended discussion of the semantic-differential technique, which is beyond the scope of this text, it must be mentioned that the findings of the technique lead to a strengthening of Likert scale measurements. If we consider our previous illustration (p. 76) for the measurement of *powerlessness,* we find that the statement is concerned with *passivity* (that is, *the individual student can do nothing*), and that our scale is based on *evaluation* (for or against) and the *intensity* or strength of this evaluation. Thus, the *evaluative, intensity,* and *activity* dimensions are clearly associated with any questions of this kind. Osgood and his colleagues suggest three sets of questions, one set for evaluating each of these dimensions, so that similarities and differences between respondents may be clearly distinguished. In constructing Likert scales, such procedures are very helpful, and students inclined to survey research should consult the Osgood text.

## STUDENT RESEARCH: CONSCIOUSNESS-RAISING AND INSTRUMENTAL ACTIVITY

The following example of research, employing the methodology covered in this chapter, is in the student's own words:

* Charles E. Osgood *et al., The Measurement of Meaning* (Urbana: University of Illinois Press, 1957).

Pamela Allen (1971) and others have argued that ideology can best be developed within a structured small-group setting. The literature on small-group studies is extensive (Mills, 1967) and will not be discussed here.

A recent example of attempts to develop group identification and awareness is the proliferation of consciousness-raising groups organized by the women's movement. On my campus alone, some twelve different groups have been organized in the past two years. Some of these groups are continuing, but most have consisted of three-week sessions meeting several times a week. The purpose of these groups is to make the participants aware of women as a distinct class or group within society and to encourage them, through directed discussion of themselves and their problems, to bring about changes in the social system that will be more equitable toward women.

In the research I performed for this class, I sought to test the efficacy of consciousness-raising groups in developing instrumental activism. By "instrumental activism" I mean activity directed toward bringing about change in the existing situations. I have purposely included the word *instrumental* to distinguish this activity from *expressive* activity. Expressive activity is emotive activity, not rationally planned action intended to manipulate the object world. The dichotomy of instrumental *vs.* expressive activity is frequently encountered in sociology. It is a carryover from the structural-functionalism of Parsons. Too often any feminist activity is seen as expressive activity by its opponents, and I therefore decided to eliminate it from my research.

In attempting to measure the efficacy of these consciousness-raising groups, I reasoned that if the group activity accomplished its intended purpose, women who had attended these groups should be engaged currently in constructive activities to change society. Therefore, if I sampled women who had attended for at least three weeks and women who had never attended, the former should be engaged in greater effort to change society. My hypothesis was as follows:

> *Attendance at consciousness-raising groups increases the degree of instrumental activity directed at social change.*

My unit of analysis was the individual woman. I compared women who had attended such groups with women who had not.

I devised a simple scale for measuring instrumental activity and applied it to each unit of analysis. A very simple research design resulted, and I was able to complete the entire research in only two weeks' time. The essential design is shown in Figure 1.

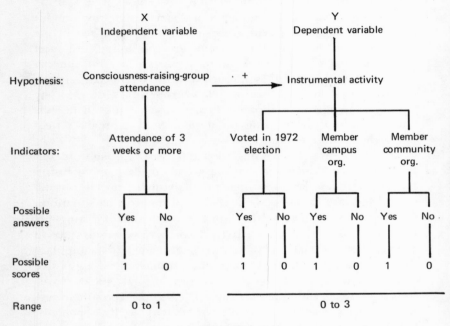

**Figure 1**

The design compares two kinds of activities as variables to be tested. By employing a simple four-item questionnaire, I was able to obtain all the information I required. It should also be noted that the use of "dummy variables" made the research, tabulation, and analysis of results very simple. Since each variable has been expressed in a way that enabled me to enter a 0 or a 1 directly onto a tally sheet, no additional coding was required.

The sampling procedure did not allow for randomization, and therefore I did not perform any statistical tests. Rather than requiring subjects to fill out forms, I simply stopped each respondent on campus and asked the following questions in the order given:

1. Did you vote in the 1972 Presidential election or in any other election that year?
2. Do you participate in any community organization, either at home or in this city?
3. Are you now or have you been a member of any campus organization?
4. Have you ever attended a women's consciousness-raising group for at least three weeks?

Since each indicator was dichotomized into a yes or no answer, I could assign a value of 0 to a "no" answer and a value of 1 to a "yes" answer. Thus my independent variable could have a range of scores from 0 to 1, while my dependent variable could range from 0 to 3. I could then further dichotomize my dependent variable scores into a "low" and a "high" score, rating a score of 0 or 1 as "low" and a score of 2 or 3 as "high."

The research hypothesis assumes that attendance at consciousness-raising groups is positively related to instrumental activity toward social change. This requires that in sampling for respondents I obtain an equal number of women in each of the two categories of the independent variable. Since I had decided before undertaking the survey to limit my total number of respondents to 60, or 30 in each category, I allowed respondents to accumulate, scoring each respondent until one category of Question 4 had reached the 30 mark. It happened that the category that first attained the 30 mark was "no"—that is, women who had not attended consciousness-raising groups. From that point on, I asked Question 4 first, selecting only those women who had attended such groups to provide an equal number of respondents and deleting any others. This happened when my total for such women was only 18.

*Procedure*

The interviewing procedure was very simple. I had made a raw-data tabulating form such as that shown in Figure 1. My procedure was to station myself on campus during class

| Question → | 1 | 2 | 3 | 4 |
|---|---|---|---|---|
| **Person** | | | | |
| 1 | 1 | 0 | 0 | 0 |
| 2 | 1 | 0 | 0 | 1 |
| 3 | 1 | 1 | 0 | 0 |
| — | 0 | 0 | 0 | 1 |
| — | 1 | 0 | 0 | 1 |
| 60 | 0 | 1 | 1 | 0 |
| **Totals:** | | | | |

Figure 2

changes and stop every third woman who passed a given point. I could ask my four questions very rapidly, since all I had to do was enter a 0 or a 1 in the appropriate column opposite the respondent. (In the example given in Figure 2, there are three women who have never attended a consciousness-raising group for at least three weeks and three who have. Person 1 has not attended but has voted, person 2 has attended but has not voted, and so forth.) The use of such "dummy variable" notation expedites the research and, I think, allows the researcher to conceptualize the research design very clearly.

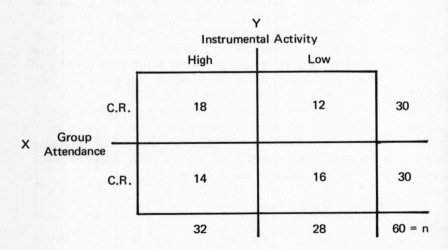

Figure 3

*Results*

The results I obtained were not what I had expected. These data are presented in Figure 3.

Each cell of the contingency table contains the number of women falling into both Y and X categories. The 30 who had not attended consciousness-raising groups $(\overline{C.R.})$ have a slightly lower cell total on high instrumental activity than on low, but this is accounted for by the score of only one person out of 30. (That is, if one of the low scorers of the C.R. category had been high instead of low, exactly half the total of 30 in this category would have been in each of the lower cells, or 15 in each instead of 14 and 16.) The 30 who had attended consciousness-raising groups (C.R.) show a more pronounced difference between cells 60 percent, or 18, engage in instrumental activity as opposed to only about 47 percent of the $\overline{C.R.}$ women. Hence, one might be tempted to conclude that consciousness-raising does indeed result in an increase in instrumental activity. Since, however, the $\overline{C.R.}$ category breaks almost equally, this conclusion must be tempered. The C.R.-low cell accounts for 40 percent of the C.R. responses, the $\overline{C.R.}$-high cell for 46 percent of the $\overline{C.R.}$ responses. I would have expected this latter cell to be much lower. What the data seem to show is that instrumental activity is relatively high for women on this campus, whether or not they have attended consciousness-raising groups. As one can see by the marginals, 32/60, or 53 percent, of *all* women scored high on instrumental activity. Although 18/30, or 60 percent, of the C.R. women scored high, this difference may be attributable primarily to the process by which women join C.R. groups in the first place. In other words, we would expect women who have been actively involved in community organizations and campus organizations and who have voted to join C.R. groups. Hence, any results we obtain should be markedly different between C.R. and $\overline{C.R.}$ if it is the group membership that is causing the involvement in instrumental activity, rather than the involvement in instrumental activity causing the group involvement. Although I was not able to reject my hypothesis, further research seems to be necessary.

## Discussion

This research attempted to show whether involvement in consciousness-raising groups increased participation in instrumental activity. Only if instrumental activity does increase can an ideology become politicized and some form of affirmative action result. This survey showed that instrumental activity by women on this campus is already quite high. Although there appears to be a greater number of women with high scores who have been consciousness raising–group members, the relative proportion of these is not greatly different from that of nongroup members. This suggests that the criteria by which women become group members require further investigation. If consciousness-raising groups attract women of high instrumentality, then this may be sufficient for politicized activity that can lead to results. The findings do, however, imply that little "conversion" takes place in the group itself. If, however, consciousness-raising groups do not primarily attract women of high instrumentality but "convert" women by raising their consciousness, then indeed a politically powerful mechanism for social change has been obtained in the consciousness-raising group.

### Suggested Readings

Backstrom, H., and Gerald Hursh, *Survey Research* (Chicago: Northwestern University Press, 1965).

Blalock, Hubert, *An Introduction to Social Research* (Englewood Cliffs, N.J.: Prentice-Hall, 1970).

Cole, Stephen, *The Sociological Method* (Chicago: Markham, 1972).

Davis, James A., *Elementary Survey Analysis* (Englewood Cliffs, N.J.: Prentice-Hall, 1971).

Forcese, Dennis P., *Social Research Methods* (Englewood Cliffs, N.J.: Prentice-Hall, 1973).

# 4

# *Participant Observation*

FROM THE TWO PRECEDING CHAPTERS, it should be apparent that content analysis and survey research are varieties of a common analytical approach. This approach was discussed in the opening chapter. Its central focus involves the definition and isolation of categories into which units of analysis are sorted according to whether they possess or lack the property specified in the category. Once these units have been collected, they are systematically compared for similarities and differences and the groups identified with respect to the relationship existing between them, the strength of that relationship, and its direction. Inferences respecting the association between the groups may then be made.

The definition of categories should be such that they are rendered mutually exclusive and exhaustive. Units of analysis must not be confused: We must compare like with like, *not* like with unlike. We must be wary of committing certain fallacies. The fallacies of reductionism, the ecological fallacy, and the others discussed in Chapter 1 await us at every turn. We should begin with a research design that stipulates what it is that we are going to prove and how we are going to go about proving it, identifying the independent and dependent variables and the expected relationship between them. We start with a hypothesis and seek to reject it by our test, but we may fail to reject it. Thus far, I have specified stating a *research hypothesis* and neglected the concept of a *null hypothesis,* for the latter is more meaningful in statistical tests of significance than in the analytical process itself. The use of statistical tests of significance are currently being questioned in the discipline and will not be elaborated upon here.

The student could profit at this point by returning to the end of Chapter 1 and rereading the section on "Concepts, Words, and Phenomena." There it was noted that words serve mediating functions between the exterior phenomena of the physical (or *object*) world and the internal, mental world of concepts (or *ideas*). Words enable one mind in a community to communicate with another mind in that community by introducing symbolic sounds into the object world, sounds denoting concepts shared by both parties in the communication. But words also shape the mind's understanding of the reality in which it finds itself, because of the central role played by language in the socialization of the young. We know that there may not be phenomena corresponding to certain concepts (such as that signified by the word *mermaid*) or to certain nonsense words. When we specify a category in our research design and then provide indicators of it by means of some operationalized definitions, can we be certain that the concept so indicated does in fact exist?

This is not an easy question to answer. The research design we employ attempts to free us from the tyranny of language by insisting that we use indicators that are capable of measuring the presence or absence of a property of the unit of analysis. Thus we detect in object space (that is, in the external world about us) those properties that we have *ourselves* identified with the concepts we employ as variables. This is all well and good, and scientifically sound. But it should be noted that once we do this our indicators are defining our concepts, and *not* our concepts defining our indicators! This may or may not be satisfactory to the researcher, depending upon his own research perspective. One could rightly argue that we have given up the attempt to define a word by other words and have ventured upon establishing sets of indcators to replace them. Thus, it may be argued that what really interests those who employ indicators is the *reproducibility* of the indicators, not the concepts for which they are supposed to stand. Many eminent sociologists maintain this position.

Other sociologists, equally eminent, find this solution unsatisfactory. They claim that by establishing indicators prior to the act of empirical research we are insisting on what *ought* to occur, not examining what in fact occurs. They agree that as long as sociology claims to be scientific and hence empirical, sociological research should first of all engage social activity in its concrete form rather than treat it as abstraction. Only by careful observation of real social situations can we obtain the kind of data required to build theory that makes any sense. At present, they assert, we have many conflicting theories that have been established wholly upon presumptions of human behavior rather than upon meticulous observation. At the same time we have a host of observations gathered in a kind of vacuum from which meanings have been eliminated. Herbert Blumer was one of the first to point out this basic failing in sociological inquiry. It has been echoed by many others.

This is not really a new issue in sociology; instead, it is the reassertion of some of the original premises of American sociology and is reflected in such works as the study by W. I. Thomas and Florian Znaniecki of *The Polish Peasant in Europe and America,* published in 1918. However, with the introduction of the translated works of Weber and Durkheim, this earlier thrust became deflected. The structural functionalism of Talcott Parsons and his followers attempted to integrate the work of such European scholars into a unified whole and for a time formed the salient school in American sociology. Although their efforts stimulated an interest in sociology in the United States and helped to bridge the gap between Continental and American social science, it also gave at least tacit support to extreme operationalism in research. Extreme operationalism, it will be recalled, sees only the indicators as real, not the concepts, which are held to be "mere words." It can be seen that the position of some sociologists—that one may sometimes neglect the concepts if the measurability and reproducibility of the indicators are high— lies dangerously close to the extreme operationalist position. While these sociologists may protest that they have, in fact, created a *construct* (such as *intelligence,* as measured by I.Q. testing), it is nevertheless true that they have replaced concept and construct alike by focusing attention solely upon their indicators. (Thus the I.Q. score of an individual is taken as communicating all that is "real" about that individual's ability to think intelligently!)

This whole matter of operationalization was introduced into modern physics by Percy W. Bridgeman in 1927. By 1939 the sociologist George A. Lundberg borrowed it for the social sciences. It seems doubtful that it would have attained such an "orthodox" position in sociology had it not been for the abstruse qualities that began to emerge in the theoretical writings of Talcott Parsons. Parsons's stress upon the normative, for example, was pronounced. Since such a concept is highly abstract, it can be detected only by indicators more concrete in meaning. Hence, many survey researchers found it expedient to employ operationalization as a means of detecting and measuring otherwise unmeasurable properties and qualities of societies. But we must remember that the fact that we have a word for a concept does not mean that a phenomenon corresponding to that word and concept must really exist. Mermaids, if they ever existed, surely exist no longer.

The principle of applying operational definitions to concepts is very useful. Its purpose is to provide indicators for measuring attributes believed to be associated with those concepts. When properly employed, this principle is capable of yielding a great deal of otherwise unobtainable information. But we must always remember that any inference we make as a result of our research design and hypotheses relates to the indicators, not to the concepts themselves. The relation between the indicators and the concepts can be ascertained only *outside* the research, by the tenets of scientific theory.

Operationalized variables and the relationship hypothesized between them are useful conceptual tools for understanding the social reality we find about us, but they must be applied judiciously. They are only a few of the many tools we have at our disposal for investigating social phenomena. Until our theoretical base is much firmer than it is at present, to insist that operationalization must be performed and that only the indicators are real certainly seems presumptuous and scarcely scientific.

The scientific method employed by Francis Bacon (1561–1626) involved observing phenomena, classifying them into categories, and descriptive analysis. Galileo (1564–1642) and Newton (1642–1727) added the idea of the crucial experiment and deductive inference. These methods sufficed for the explanation of the immediate physical world, the world as experienced in its physical nature. The emergence of modern physics in the early part of the twentieth century met the need for scientific knowledge beyond that of immediate physical objects, supplying relativistic and statistical tools for its exploration. In their efforts to establish social inquiry as a science, social thinkers began borrowing the methods of modern physics. But it is becoming increasingly apparent that this was a mistake. There was not a sufficient explanation of the immediate *social* reality of the kind attained by Bacon, Galileo, and Newton of the immediate *physical* reality. There are doubts that this is even possible. Confronted with the unproductivity and unpredictability of their own efforts, social scientists jumped to statistical measures, hoping that predictability (which they saw as crucial to the notion of science) might improve. It has not done so.

Moreover, predictability in the absence of a theoretical base can hardly generate meaning and understanding. The meaning of social action is the ultimate goal of social inquiry. Such meaning can emerge only from a detailed observation of what social action does in fact consist of. Hence, many contemporary sociologists argue for a return to a more descriptive sociology, one based upon active participation by the sociologist as observer. This is none the less scientific; observation, classification, and descriptive analysis and deductive inference are, as we saw, the basis of the scientific method, and a great deal of survey research ignores observation entirely and substitutes operationalization instead.

The student who has experimented with the methods described thus far is well prepared for the sociologist-as-participant methods of this chapter. The techniques of participant observation are, however, less formally organized and defined than those of the previous methods. For this reason, the student should become acquainted with such classical participant-observation studies as William F. Whyte's *Street Corner Society* and Howard Becker's *Outsiders*. Some more recent examples are Jerry Jacobs's *Fun*

*City* and *Adolescent Suicide;* the latter is interesting in that it combines open-ended interview techniques with insights gained from content analysis of suicide notes, two of the techniques we have been discussing.

## VARIETIES OF PARTICIPANT OBSERVATION

At the present time there appear to be several varieties of participant observation that have gained acceptance as viable techniques of sociological research. Among these are studies dealing with *ethnographies,* descriptive accounts similar to those produced by anthropologists. Just as anthropologists study primitive peoples by observation, note-taking, and interviewing to determine the patterns binding the group together, so the ethnographic participant observer attempts to understand some group or community. This necessarily calls for a suspension, on his part, of whatever preconceived ideas he may have had of the group's beliefs or of the reasons behind particular modes of behavior. It also requires that he condition himself to suppress outward signs of disapproval, disgust, or surprise and seek to observe with the eyes of those whose activity he is studying. Many teachers of participant observation insist that at all times and in all situations the sociologist must attempt to maintain objectivity in order to retain observational clarity. This brings about a paradoxical situation: One must remain aloof in order to perceive what is "in fact" happening, while simultaneously attempting to take the viewpoint of those others whose structured life situation is being studied. This variety of participant observation proposes two basic principles, which point to the quixotic position in which the participant observer is placed:

- Don't go native or your objectivity will be lost.
- Remain skeptical of your objectivity. Objectify yourself in relation to your respondents; remember that your role as outsider affects the responses of others and of yourself.*

To "go native" is to accept and internalize the mores, norms,

---

* Adapted from Arthur Vidich, "Participant Observation and the Collection and Interpretation of Data," in William J. Filstead, *Qualitative Methodology* (Chicago: Markham, 1970).

beliefs, habits, and practices of the studied group.* Mr. Kurtz, in Conrad's *Heart of Darkness,* "goes native" and is unable to extricate himself from the alien culture. One way of avoiding going native is to employ marginal individuals in the group, people who think of themselves as "not really" a part of the group, although they are indeed part of it, if in a less central manner than some others. In studying hospital situations, for example, where one is interested in the structure of authority binding physicians and surgeons together, one may learn a great deal from nurses and orderlies that could not possibly be obtained from the physicians and surgeons themselves. Such marginal persons are bridges to the meanings, values, and norms of the society; by listening to them and observing their inter-actions with the central figures involved, one may learn a great deal about the structure and organization of the situations. The nurses and orderlies are at a shorter social distance from the physicians and surgeons than the sociologist is as an outsider. But they are close enough to be entangled in the web of mean-ings, authority, and stratification the situations involve. Re-member that *the greater the social distance between the observer and the observed, the less adequate the communication between them.*

But why are we observing these situations to begin with? We are looking for that concept, or group of concepts, that binds the particular group we are studying into a small society. We are attempting to understand what everyday life is to the people who are living it, what they take for granted as real and unchallengeable in their daily existence. By careful note-taking of our observations of actions, recording bits of dialogue and theoretical insights as they occur to us, we hope to be able to discover a pattern that is applicable to the group as a whole and possibly (by extension) to the larger society as a whole. We are, in short, attempting to get at the basic material of which societies are formed. Our task here is observation; from such observation, insights may (or may not) emerge. Just as Galileo and Newton performed innumerable observations, hoping to detect a pattern within them, so do we. We, like they, seek the *nomothetic* (the *generalizable*). We do this by

* Although there are participant-observation methodologists who do in-deed "go native," their techniques are not recommended for the beginner.

trying to discern those *iterative* (or *repeatable*) patterns that occur in many discrete, separate, and individual events (that is, in the *idiographic*). This may not be completely clear to the student and is worth some extended discussion here.

In my efforts to describe content analysis and survey research, I was trying to establish some broad, generalizable principles. In seeking to discern whether freshmen or seniors were more alienated, for example, we concerned ourselves with three broad categories (freshmen, seniors, alienation) and tried to determine some relationship among them. We felt that this relationship involved certain broad principles of integration, applicable to many individuals in a society, not just to the specific people we met on campus. This does not mean that we denied the uniqueness of the actual occurrences involving real individuals. All activity, all experience, is unique: It did not occur previously. Indeed, this is precisely why historians study events: to discern their unique character. Any action that occurs in the world of real people is uniquely placed in time, in that it occurs at a new moment, a moment that never was. Each of us is constantly undergoing alteration, and no two of us are experiencing this in exactly the same manner, for we are each located differently in space. This difference in location places each of us in a separate and distinct environment, shared by no other. All events that occur, therefore, are *idiographic* (that is, unique, individual, unusual, particularistic).

But social scientists, although granting this fact, claim that it does not preclude the individual event from being part of a pattern, structure, or process that is common to a whole class of such events. Since it is only this larger, more general pattern that interests the sociologist, sociology differs from history in its emphasis upon the nomothetic, the generalizing and patterning of events. Most sociologists agree that the greater part of behavior (if not all behavior) is *learned behavior,* despite its complexity and nonpredictability, and that, quite apart from the uniqueness of occurrence, there are in addition some properties that apply to that whole class of occurrences.

Hence, what most participant observers search for are those more general properties, such as *role, norm, structure, hierarchy, stratification, contract, exchange,* and the like. Precisely what is searched for is, of course, wholly dependent upon the theoret-

earlier in the chapter. See whether he knows what's going on. Record his opinions and check them against your own.

• Whenever anything occurs to you that you feel is directly related to your research observations, no matter where you are, write it down.

• Constantly examine your categories. Modify them if you think they are no longer meaningful or if a better scheme begins to emerge from the data. Follow your hunches. A good hunch may lead to a far better research design than the one you began with. Do not be afraid to modify your design, but do not discard anything. Although you may be working according to some revised design, be certain that your old design and the notes resulting from it are available; reread them constantly. Do not be afraid to challenge the fidelity of your categories, even those most taken for granted in your sociologically oriented thinking.

• Look for emerging patterns of structured relationships.

• Don't go native! If necessary, seek to alienate yourself from the situation in order to obtain the objectivity required to understand what is going on. Try to write down the viewpoint of the others, but don't *believe* it. Try to see the situation as they see it, but don't *believe* what you see. Acknowledge to yourself that *they* believe it, and remember that you would expect them to respect what you believe were they observing you. Do not challenge their beliefs.

• When all field notes have been completed (and this will be determined by the length of time available to pursue the research as much as by anything else), retrace the steps you took and the changes that have occurred in your hypotheses and categories. If your observational notes are fairly complete, you will have noted various cases of apparently illogical occurrences, unexpected behaviors, and these will have led you, one hopes, to focus upon peculiar or unusual attributes of what occurs in these situations. It is here that the greatest discoveries can be made. To find patterned interactional phenomena that, while not logical, exhibit an internal consistency and rationale of their own is one of the principal goals of participant observation. It may be that you will end by throwing away the categories you started with, as well as your previous notions of *norms,*

*ends-means,* and the like. This is all well and good. In writing
the report this development must be mentioned. Any set of
observations that render previous assumptions invalid or challenge accepted theories is scientifically valuable. What you are
looking for, after all, is *meaning.* If one can determine the
meanings held by actors in social situations and the manner in
which these meanings either determine behavior or are determined by it, one has confronted the center of the sociological
problem.

## WRITING THE REPORT

The best advice on writing the report is obtained by studying
the work of professionals, particularly those mentioned earlier
in this chapter. It is important to remember the nomothetic
principle enunciated earlier: We search for principles of general
applicability even when we examine specific instances. What
we observe should be applicable to a greater number of cases
and kinds of situations than those we have observed: It should
be typical of what occurs when situations are structured as they
were when we made our observations. In writing the report we
try to express *why* the events observed occurred in the manner
they did. But the *why* need not satisfy our own logic as it must
whatever "logic" is operating in the situation, no matter how
irrational it may seem. Many student reports of participation
observation that I have seen reflect the prejudices of the student's
middle-class background and his associated hang-ups. They read
as if the student were rebelling against his class origins by
allowing the focus of his attention to be drawn to what his parents
would have found objectionable. While a certain amount of
this is unavoidable, excessive preoccupation with one's own background assumptions, when this is revealed in the report, detracts
from the research. Remember that there is a difference between
social science and journalism, and that you are writing for
scholars, not for the readers of the *New York Daily News.* Your
goal is not to amuse, shock, mortify, or outrage your reader. Your
goal is to set down, in as objective a manner as possible, those
details and sets of relationships that seem to occur regularly in
the class of situation you have studied.

Your report should begin with a broad description of the

research, the kind of terrain in which it was conducted, and a statement respecting the goals initially sought and their sociological importance. The initial and final forms of any hypotheses should be stated, and then an account given that is as faithful to the situation as you can make it. Obviously some people write better than others. Some have a good nose for clues, while others can follow up very well once clues have been found. It is important to point out each major challenge to your assumptions as it occurred and the manner in which it was resolved. A direct, literal account of the major form the interaction takes is very important. To obtain this in writing it may be necessary to take the larger picture first, describe it, and then gradually narrow down your focus and scope to the particular act, or group of acts, that you feel is most characteristic of the phenomenon itself.

You may feel that you can do most justice to your observations by setting them down as a scenario or short story. Do this, by all means, if it is most comfortable. But don't let your imagination run away; in writing short stories the plot often develops beyond the control of the author. This frequently makes for an excellent short story but poor sociology. The writer of an ethnography or of any participant-observation account must be in complete, conscious control of what he is setting down. Inspiration, if it occurs at all, should ideally take place during the observing process and the period of analysis, *before* writing starts and prior to the conclusion of the research. This separates science from creative writing, sociology from journalism.

Any research, to be sociologically relevant, should finally relate to those categories that are theoretically useful and applicable to a wide range of situations. The mundane, the ordinary, the taken-for-granted, need not be sociologically trivial, for this is the stuff of which social life is composed. The research should not, however, be trivial at the level of *theory;* if it is, it contributes nothing to our understanding, no matter how complex are the techniques that have been used.

Ultimately, of course, you will find yourself returning to the same principles of analysis that have been stressed throughout this book. Look for the definition and isolation of categories and observe carefully the number of instances falling into these categories. Systematically compare these categories for

similarities and differences, the strength and direction of relationships, before attempting to make any distinctions with respect
to the meanings these might have for participants. When you
feel that you have exhausted all possibilities and possible alternatives, begin the report. In writing it, strive to communicate the
essentials of your analytical process.

Before closing this chapter with an example of student research, a few warnings are necessary:

Beware the *holistic fallacy.* The fact that two things occur
at the same time does not mean that they are necessarily
connected with each other. To put this in another way, the fact
that something is observed in a particular situation does not
mean that the something is a product or quality of that
situation. There is a marked tendency to see everything in
connection with the situation covered. To see cannibals dancing
about a kettle on the fire does not mean that they dance because
a kettle is on the fire. Also, it does not mean that they are about
to boil a missionary. They may have heard some good news at
the moment of your observation and, there being no other
clearing in the forest than the one in which the kettle was cook-
ing, decided to dance there. Only repeated observations of
cannibals, kettles, and dances can show whether they are somehow connected. Kettles are properties of many other social
situations, and so are dances. While it may be difficult to ignore
preconceptions about the association of kettles and cannibals,
based upon one's own socialization, these must be thrust aside
and the situation examined in terms of what does occur, not
what one thinks ought to occur. And what is occurring is not
easy to see, for we see through the eyes furnished us by our
language and socialization processes. If we continually strive
for objectivity in perceiving what actually does occur, participant-
observation methods can help to challenge some of the unwarranted assumptions that have crept into our social thought.
But we must be careful in seeing. We must make certain that
we can reduce the situation to the elements composing it by
constantly rechecking our categories and hypotheses. An activity
that is present at the time of the phenomenon may not be an
element of that phenomenon and, therefore, must be excluded
from our description of the phenomenon.

Another warning is necessary regarding the abuses of the

notion of *verstehen.* This notion, which originated in the writings of Georg Simmel and was popularized by Max Weber, is invaluable from the standpoint of social theory. However, it is very difficult to employ and should not be used indiscriminately. *Verstehen,* the German word for "to understand," approaches the form of a construct in some sociological writings. It is often claimed that, because the observer is a socialized human being and the targets of his observations are socialized human beings, he has a methodological advantage over the physical scientist, who must deal with objects of a different kind from himself. Presented in this way, the argument implies that I can understand what I see of human activity simply because I, too, am human. This is patent nonsense. *Verstehen,* in this sense, simply means that I *guess* what you have in mind. I can, of course, be wrong in my guess, and very often I am; I misunderstand you and you misunderstand me more often than either of us likes to admit. Indeed, it is just such failures in communication between individuals that makes the methodology of participant observation possible. Definitions of situations are not homogeneous, particularly under conditions of great social change, when individual expectations of reciprocal behavior are not ratified by performance. The identity I symbolically announce to you by my dress, speech, and behavior may not be interpreted by you in the manner I intend or would like. You may take these as signs of something other than I take them as, for in times of change the *signs* are up for grabs: Standards in dress, manner, speech, and behavior are relaxed. To put this conversely, I may dress in a particular way in order to convince myself that I am a particular type of person, and I may find reinforcement for this view of myself in the reactions of others with whom I interact, who interpret these signs as I do. Knowledge of this principle has existed for some time: Advertisers and clothing manufacturers thrive on it, as do the manufacturers and vendors of cosmetics, deodorants, automobiles, and related consumer products. The whole matter of announcing one's identity and presenting one's self in a certain set of standardized symbols is brilliantly explored by Erving Goffman.* The point I am making here is that we can understand social phenomena only

* Erving Goffman, *The Presentation of Self in Everyday Life* (Garden City, N.Y.: Doubleday, 1959).

by prolonged, careful, and controlled observation—only by looking at what appear to be unalterable qualities or properties of those phenomena. When we are convinced that those phenomena behave in certain ways and no others, *then* we understand. This is precisely what the physical scientist does. The inert matter of his observations puts up *fewer* false fronts, not *more*. The living human target of our observations may or may not feel satisfied that he or she knows who he or she *is;* personal identity, in terms of inherited roles and role expectations, is difficult to come by in times of great social change. He or she may assume a variety of identities, announcing them differently under different circumstances. Our problem, as observers, is to pierce through these "disguises," if possible. This may not always *be* possible. But the *effort* is possible, and it is worth our performing on the chance that we may, indeed, be right, and may learn something sociologically useful as a result.

STUDENT RESEARCH: PARTICIPANT OBSERVATION OF ALCOHOLICS ANONYMOUS

The following example of research, employing the methodology covered in this chapter, is in the student's own words:

This report presents some of the conclusions drawn from my own participant-observation studies of self-therapy groups. These studies were conducted over a single semester. Twelve sessions of Alcoholics Anonymous were attended. These were "open" meetings to which the public was invited, and at no time did I ever pretend to be an alcoholic in order to attend. Those people who asked why I was attending (and they were few) were told of my student interest in learning about group processes.

The purpose of my study was twofold. I wanted to learn something about participant observation as a technique of social research. In addition, I wanted to test Simmel's thesis that people in very large cities develop blasé attitudes as a way of dealing with the many stimuli present. I had reasoned that such an attitude should make metropolitan groups of Alcoholics Anonymous less meaningful to participants than similar groups in small towns are to their participants. I wanted to see whether what went on at the meetings of these relatively intimate groups depended upon whether they took place in Metropolis or Small

Town. Metropolis is a city of several million people. Small Town is a community of about 50,000, just outside University Town, where I attend college. I attended six groups in Small Town and six in Metropolis. (I should really have attended more sessions of each group, but there was not enough time in a single semester.) The detailed notes I took are included in a separate appendix; * in this part of the report all I want to do is present a discussion of my findings.

In his essay on "The Metropolis and Mental Life," Georg Simmel spends considerable time discussing the fact that the big city presents so many stimuli to the resident, not only visual but aural, that the resident must build up a defense against them or be overwhelmed by them and unable to live there. He is constantly exposed to horrible sights and suffering, and if he takes them at all seriously, as people do in small towns, his coping limits will be exceeded. Therefore he develops a blasé attitude, ignoring most of the stimuli about him and selecting only those aspects of his environment that are of direct and immediate concern to himself.

Symbols of personal identity become much more important to the big-city person, and he is forced to judge the identity of others by the external symbols of dress and manner that they affect. He "screens out" those who are not wearing the appropriate uniforms of identification. All his interactions with others are likely to be on a relatively superficial level. He is compelled to isolate himself from others for privacy, since there is so little physical privacy in the city and one way to obtain it is to ignore even your next-door neighbor in the apartment house. This is very different from the case in a small town, where everybody knows everybody else, or at least knows who and what they are, and there is a common communal concern. An automobile accident in a small town, one involving physical injury to people, is discussed by everyone in town for many days. In the big city, however, so many accidents occur that no one pays very much attention to them: If people did, they would have no time for living.

I formulated a hypothesis from reading the essays by Simmel that we had been assigned in class. This hypothesis was the

* The appendix the student refers to is not reprinted here; it is very long and would make a small book by itself.

starting point of my research. I hypothesized that the larger the city, the more formal would be the conduct of residents when they were participants in small groups. Since AA (Alcoholics Anonymous) is composed of small groups of persons meeting regularly in face-to-face interaction with a common bond to unite them, it should be possible to compare groups as units of analysis and see how much difference exists between AA groups in small towns and AA groups in big cities. Ideally, one should also compare these with AA groups in rural areas, but these are limited in number and not very accessible to me.

## Procedures

I attended the meetings of two groups each week. These usually start at about 8 P.M. and run for about two hours. At most of these meetings participants sit around a long table with the speaker for the evening at the head of the table. He recounts his past problems, particularly as these were associated with alcoholism, and tells how and why he stopped drinking. Then they go around the table, with each person either speaking or passing. If he speaks, a person gives his first name and identifies himself as an alcoholic, then a short discussion of the speaker's talk as it relates to his own problem with alcohol. Then the next person speaks. At some meetings, the speaker for the evening calls upon people to talk: "John, tell us about your situation." There is a great deal of flexibility in procedure, but the basic mechanism is the same. There is a lead speaker; then the discussion passes to people sitting about the table, with most of those who speak beginning by stating their names and the fact that they are alcoholics. This identification of oneself as an alcoholic, even if one has not had a drink in years, is part of the AA program. There are others present, just beginning the program, who do not like to consider themselves alcoholics, and sometimes these people speak, too, or question what others have said. However, it is not my object here to discuss the AA program and its operation. What I was concerned with in my observations was possible differences between Metropolis and Small Town groups, where these groups were similar in size, purpose, and program. I expected Small Town groups to be more informal than Metropolis groups and to contain a great deal more emotional warmth and understanding.

I found that in Small Town most group members came from outside the town itself, some from University Town and its suburbs. People never used their family names, and never in speaking with each other did they identify too closely the street where they lived or the specific jobs they held. The big attraction of AA for them, aside from the central fact that they recognized that they had drinking problems, was the anonymous quality associated with group participation. If one was an alcoholic, one could come here to discuss a common problem and be certain that it would not be found out and become a topic of gossip in one's own town or neighborhood. Very few people came from the immediate area in which the meetings were held. Many traveled a considerable distance by car. Since meetings were in the evening, almost all were neatly dressed, however casual and suburban their clothing. Most spoke well, and many seemed to be well educated. The women seemed more reluctant than the men to identify themselves as alcoholics. No one ever employed suggestive language.

There is usually a coffee break part way through the meeting at AA sessions. At these breaks the people in Small Town groups would chat with others they knew from their attendance at the meetings. Strangers or newcomers were seldom spoken to the first few times they came; indeed, I found that the first time I went to any Small Town meeting the participants glanced at me discreetly, perhaps with a slight smile, but did not attempt to engage me in conversation. However, if I as a newcomer spoke to them, they would respond and hold a conversation with me. They would seldom ask where I was from; some recognized that I must be a student and asked, but these were very few. In general, they tended to be very discreet in their interactions with each other, even with those they knew from visiting other meetings in the area.

I found the situation in Metropolis to be very different. At the very first group I attended, people asked me where I lived, and it startled me. When I told them, they suggested that I attend a group much closer to my home. At first I thought they wanted to discourage my attendance, but I soon found out that they all lived within a block of the meeting place. At other meetings in Metropolis the same phenomenon was observed. Although some people traveled a distance to be present, almost all came from the immediate neighborhood. Since there are many more groups in Metropolis than in Small Town, I found this difficult to understand.

People in Metropolis freely exchanged addresses, names, and phone numbers and did not feel at all self-conscious about entering the AA meeting place or even lingering outside on the sidewalk when the meeting was over. Also, they did not all get dressed up for the meetings; some came immediately from work and wore whatever they had worn to work. Since there was much more diversity of occupation in Metropolis than in Small Town, not everyone was dressed casually or even neatly. In the groups I attended in Metropolis, most of the people were well educated, too, but they tended to use more direct language, including a great deal of what the Small Town participants would have considered profanity. But, in addition, their insights seemed much more profound and meaningful, much less sprinkled with irrelevancies than those of the Small Town participants. I knew that both groups work—that is, both groups have good records when it came to terminating alcoholism among members. But it seemed to me that what I had expected to find was not at all evident. If anything, the interactions of the Metropolis participants were far less formal than those of Small Town participants. In addition, the Metropolis people, who had relative anonymity as Metropolis residents, seemed to be capable of far more intense and honest interaction with others of their kind than did the Small Town people, who had little anonymity in their places of residence. My initial hypothesis did not hold. I found the reverse of what I had expected.

I have no doubt that Simmel's concept of the blasé attitude is valid, and I have seen sufficient evidence of it on the street. I know that many of the people I met at the Metropolis meetings carry such an attitude with them when they are not at AA meetings. But I have seen them in the street, shopping, walking their dogs, and coming from work. If they recognize you from a meeting, they will stop and talk with you. Conversely, if I met someone from a Small Town meeting in a similar situation, they would not stop; an occasional nod was all I ever received.

As this occurred to me, I hypothesized that the AA meetings might provide a release from strain for alcoholics. Under such an assumption, a Metropolis alcoholic might find tension release by abandoning the anonymity thrust upon him by Metropolis, while a Small Towner might find tension release in the (for him) unusual anonymity of the AA meeting—that is, by obtaining anonymity. This could mean that whatever Small Town pressures result in alcoholism or whatever Metropolis pressures do, the face-to-face interaction format provides tension release by bringing people together in a form that is in opposition to that in which they usually live. The Metropolitan person escapes from the blasé attitude and the Small Towner is brought to it. In either case, it is the "unnatural" or "unusual" situation represented by the AA meeting that may account for the role it plays in the lives of its members. It may be that the extent to which AA becomes a part of such members' lives is related to their success in the program. Certainly those who do not make AA a part of their lives do not seem to meet much success in fighting alcoholism.

## Conclusion

This report leaves many questions unanswered, but this is because my results were not what I had predicted. I found interaction patterns in small AA groups in Metropolis to be less formal than those in Small Town. But since interaction patterns in Metropolis *generally* are more formal than in Small Town, even in small groups of a nontherapeutic kind, a great deal of additional work remains to be done. Perhaps the unusual nature of the AA meeting itself may provide release from the strain of anonymity or may provide anonymity, depending upon whether or not anonymity is conferred upon residents by their daily life-style. Both small town and big city perform a kind of deprivation of privacy, although in different ways. The AA group restores privacy. Perhaps that is why it works.

SUGGESTED READINGS

Ball, Norman W., "An Abortion Clinic Ethnography," in Jack Douglas (ed.), *Observation of Deviance* (New York: Random House, 1970).

Becker, Howard, *Outsiders* (New York: Free Press, 1963).

Blumer, Herbert, *Symbolic Interactionism* (Englewood Cliffs, N.J.: Prentice-Hall, 1969).

Bruyn, Severyn T., *The Human Perspective in Sociology* (Englewood Cliffs, N.J.: Prentice-Hall, 1966).

Filstead, William J. (ed.), *Qualitative Methodology* (Chicago: Markham, 1970).

Jacobs, Jerry, "Symbolic Bureaucracy: A Case Study of a Social Welfare Agency," *Social Forces,* 47, 1969.

Schatzman, Leonard, and Anselm Strauss, *Field Research* (Englewood Cliffs, N.J.: Prentice-Hall, 1973).

Sieber, Sam D., "The Integration of Fieldwork and Survey Methods," *American Journal of Sociology,* 78 (May, 1973).

Vidich, Arthur J., Joseph Bensman, and Maurice Stein, *Reflections on Community Studies* (New York: Wiley, 1964).

# III

# Other Methods and Other Problems

# 5

# *Historiographic Research*

IN PART II WE COVERED three principal types of research: content analysis, survey research, and participant observation. We employed the same mode of analysis in all these. We made constant comparisons *between* and *within* categories and looked for similarities and differences. These three methodologies are basic to an understanding of the results of researches one finds in the published literature, and the student would do well to work mentally back and forth among these methods as he reads the results obtained by others. In this way the basic research process will become so well established in the student's understanding that he may be able to adapt it to his central interest in sociology. Merely to ape the efforts of others is ultimately unsatisfactory and unsatisfying. Although a certain amount of imitation is required in learning, the performance of any activity soon becomes boring routine if one is not able to add a distinctive flair of one's own. This is particularly true in social research, where results are frequently less than expected. The research can become an enjoyable adventure rather than a tiresome task only if the researcher can pursue it eagerly; the best road to enthusiasm is innovation of one's own.

The preceding chapters have equipped the student with conceptual tools for exploring the social world about him. In this and the following chapters we will touch upon several additional approaches to sociological research and other techniques for employing those we have already mastered.

One technique that immediately comes to mind is historiographic analysis. In sociology such analysis usually searches for the emergence in history of some crucial idea or value, or traces the changes in meaning that have occurred respecting some commonly held concept. Remember that, as sociology is nomothetically inclined, it is not satisfied with the idiographic approach of the historians. It seeks generalizable principles of society, not unique occurrences in society; it is interested in determining principles applicable to an entire *class* of events, not to a single event.

However, a warning is required. Only the most experienced student researcher, one who is very well versed in sociological theory and method and who has, in addition, some background in history and philosophy, should undertake sociological historiographic research. This is asking for quite a bit. Such a student would probably find Chapter 2 more interesting than the succeeding two chapters, since content analysis deals with books and written materials. One must have a real love for books and documents to do historiográphic research; a great deal of the researcher's time is spent in libraries, not only those on campus but in the most out-of-the-way places, for one must work with *primary sources* whenever possible. Primary sources are *original* sources—wills, tax records, manuscripts, old maps, deeds, first editions in the original language (not translations), handwritten memoranda, memoirs, and the like. Of course, this may not always be so difficult as it sounds. The student researcher of Chapter 2, who performed the content analysis of *Time* magazine covers, worked from primary sources; in his case, primary sources were the magazine covers, and he examined one for each week in a twenty-year period. One of the foremost American sociologists, Robert K. Merton, attempted to trace the change in occupational interests among the English elite of the seventeenth century by recourse to a *secondary* source, the *Dictionary of National Biography*. These volumes, found in all university libraries, contain highly authoritative accounts of the lives of celebrated English personalities. By noting their birth dates, computing the years they probably entered their professions, and noting the professions they entered, Merton tried to trace the shift to science and technology as this field emerged. The study is an interesting attempt to get around the need for primary sources; however, it ignores whatever criteria the editors of the *Dictionary* employed in choosing the specific biographies to be included in the volume. While the student historiographer can take some consolation from the thought that Merton produced worthwhile research results without primary sources, the student's efforts should be guided by the strictest rules of scholarship. It is doubtful that the student will undertake so grandiose a research project, but projects connected with the origins of his own town or family, or some aspect of American history more accessible to him, may yield worthwhile results. Kai Erikson's book *Wayward Puritans* * is an example of such research on a more restricted scale.

In his book Erikson looks at the Salem witch trials and two other miscarriages of justice among the early Puritans. By consulting the records on convictions and arrests, he is able to show that the offender rate remained essentially constant. This suggests that societies may need a certain quota of deviants and that they may function in such a way that this quota is kept intact. Hence, deviance may be a normal phenomenon that helps to maintain group integration. This thesis is fundamental to the sociology of Emile Durkheim.

In Max Weber's classical study *The Protestant Ethic and the Spirit of Capitalism*, an attempt was made to relate the emergence of modern capitalism to the development of Puritanism. The Calvinist work ethic is found to have provided ideological support to the commercial practices emerging in England and the United States in the seventeenth and eighteenth centuries. In a related work, *Religion and the Rise of Capitalism*, R. H. Tawney traced this thesis further back into European medievalism. Complementing these efforts is Benjamin Nelson's *The Idea of Usury*, a more recent inquiry into the ancient notion of universal brotherhood and its transformation into "universal otherhood" for the purposes of economic exploitation.

It can be seen that most of these works trace the change of focus with the passage of time or stress associated with some fundamen-

---

* Kai T. Erikson, *Wayward Puritans* (New York: Wiley, 1966).

tal idea. An underlying theoretical assumption of such research is that once an idea becomes structured in a society, it will persist in its emergent form unless challenged by a competing ideology. This approach, usually termed *historicism,* is highly speculative and is most useful for suggesting possibilities rather than determining social facts. Since many possible patterns can be imposed upon past events by the synthesizing mind of the analyst, one is never able to determine what *did* take place in the past, only what *might have* taken place. To put this in another way, we do not have access to all the events of the past, only to those selected by previously living persons as significant to them and hence recorded by them. History is, after all, the pattern imposed upon events by an organizing mind; it is not an item-by-item chronology of randomly occurring events. Unless we do have such a chronology, most of the events that actually occurred in the past are lost to us. The fragments that remain may not contain the most significant data required for us to understand the reality of another time. Indeed, it appears to be patently impossible to understand the reality of any time but our own, and not even this latter reality is thoroughly understood. We are trapped today in a web of meanings as tenacious as those of the past. The most the historicist can do is attempt to evaluate previous perceptions of the world of social reality by studying the records left behind, mindful that these records have been preselected by those living in the past and "slanted" to reveal a particular ideological content to us. The problem is to see through this "slanting" wherever possible and attempt to understand the taken-for-granted assumptions couched within it.

It is apparent that the objectivity demanded of the participant observer in field research is directly comparable to that demanded of the historical researcher. Both must attempt to clear their minds of preconceptions in order to comprehend a reality other than their own. Both strive to penetrate the reality of others, whether these others are involved in interactional phenomena before them or are the authors of diaries, descriptions, or almanacs. The historical researcher, in attempting to reconstruct the past in terms of *its* meanings rather than his own, must look for the same unintentionally revealed symbols and symptoms that the field researcher seeks. He must look for what remains unexplained and taken for granted by the authors he is reading, for the appearance of irrational or noncausally related assertions, and for the ordinary, mundane, trivial, and obvious.

His task is made more complex by his displacement in time from the context of events he is studying. This is not a trivial distinction. As one example of the problem involved, consider the fact that at any time but our own the occurrence of death was far more frequent and familiar. By the time a person reached the age of twenty, he would have witnessed the deaths of many close relatives and friends and hence would contemplate his own death as a very real possibility. Death is a familiar topic in early children's readers and inspirational poetry. In contrast, the child of today sees little of death except as television fantasy, and the entire topic is avoided in child rearing in those societies where life spans have been extended. Even among mature adults in the United States, for example, there are no longer mechanisms for realistic discussions of mortality, such as those present in the extended family and religious orientations of the past. Death comes as a shock to most of us. Funerals tend to be awkward, embarrassing affairs. We have shut death out of our minds to such an extent that its occurrence stuns us. The young man or woman of today can look forward to so many years of life that the possibility of death is unthinkable. At no other time than our own was this true. The likelihood of one's own death was very real and conditioned a great part of the individual's present actions as well as his plans for the future. The idea of an after-life was far more meaningful to most people and religious bonds were far stronger than is the case today.

Displaced in time from such real concerns, the modern researcher will find difficulty in understanding the extent to which they shaped perceptions of reality. It may very well be impossible for us to understand it fully. But the attempt must be made if the historical researcher is to elicit anything of meaning.

## Selecting a Theme

As in other social research, one must begin by defining the set of relationships to be investigated. While it is probable that hypotheses will emerge from the research as one progresses, absence of an initial hypothesis means that one is fishing around, hoping that something (perhaps anything!) will turn up. It seldom does. One should have a clear idea of what is being sought before venturing forth to find it. As in field research, it may happen that once the work is under way the researcher's attention will shift to a pattern he did not expect and could not have predicted before beginning. Making discoveries is certainly the most rewarding aspect of research of any kind, and hence the original hypothesis may be discarded completely when this occurs. But a new hypothesis must suggest itself before the previous one is completely abandoned. Otherwise one might become lost in a maze of disconnected trivia that may be fascinating in themselves but cannot lead to any generalizable principle. A good research design is necessary before one begins, and it is suggested that it follow the format previously described, specifying the concepts employed, the expected relationship between them, and the indicators of those concepts.

In performing historiographic research from the standpoint of social theory, it is best to select a theme associated with one's own interests. For the beginner, the theme must be capable of exploration in one's native language; in our case, this restricts us to British and American themes. More specifically, unless the student is British by birth, it means local research in the United States employing documents written in English.

If one is tempted to undertake "grand" research in the manner of Tawney or Weber, tracing the developments in meaning of a social activity, one must remember that the word or words used to designate the phenomenon as a concept are not the same in America as in England. Such differences in meaning are due to differences in the communal experiences of the distinct national groups. At the time of the development of the railroads, for example, England was a heavily industralized nation, while the United States was primarily expanding westward into grazing land. The introduction of the steam locomotive occurred at the time of the cowboy in the United States, but England at this time was carding and spinning wool. The front piece of the locomotive, which sweeps the track clean, therefore became known as a *cowcatcher* in the United States but a *rake* in England. Here we have two different words, capable of evoking vastly different images, to designate the same item. As a contrast, consider what can occur in the meaning of the *same* word with the passage of time. The word *jazz* originally was synonymous with other slang words in English as a euphemism for sexual intercourse. One spoke of "jazzing" one's sexual partner. Later, the word came to designate a form of dancing then considered highly erotic: One symbolically "jazzed" one's dancing partner, making body movements suggesting sexual activity. Later still, *jazz* became associated with the type of music appropriate to such activity; dancing by that time was performed less frequently to jazz music than to *swing* music. Most recently, the word *jazz* has come to mean noisy and irrelevant material ("all that jazz!"). Its intermediate meaning as a word specifying a certain style of music does not seem to have fully disappeared, however. Currently the word *screw* seems to be embarked upon a related career in meaning change; similarly, the word for dance music that replaced *jazz*, the word *swing*, has acquired sexual connotations not apparent in its earlier usage.

Thus, we can have more than one word designating a concept corresponding to some phenomenon, and a specific word may designate different phenomena at different times in its usage. If we are to trace the development of a particular concept in history, we must be aware that the occurrence of a particular word may not signify the concept we understand by that word and hence may not designate the kind of activity we have specified in our research design. And it is *activity* that is of paramount interest to us, not words or even concepts. The domain of the social is an action and interactional domain, not a thought domain. We do wish not to descend to the level of mentalism or psychologism, but to remain at the level of meaningful *action*.

One may be interested in the substitution of the designating term *teenager* for the word *adolescent* in the pop culture of our own time. Of course, even the word *adolescent* is relatively new in English and marks the emergence of the idea of an intermediate phase of life between childhood and adulthood unknown in preindustrial times. What does the move toward employing the term *teenager* imply, or the terms *young adult* and *teeny-bopper*? Are the phases of life continually fragmenting to smaller and smaller increments? Why? How? Does this tell us anything about our own conception of life? Is this process an *integrating* activity or a *differentiating* activity? Does it have implications in terms of Mannheim's *problem of the generations* or in the *division of labor,* which so interested Durkheim and Marx? What are the implications?

Before we can attempt to answer such questions, we must define some historical period in which, we presume, the meanings we now have associated with such an expression as *teenager* or *teeny-bopper* did not exist, or in which the activities of persons in the age groups so designated were insufficiently different from contingent groups to set them apart as separate categories. Probably the 1940's would suffice for these particular concepts. These years are sufficiently remote in the experience of most student researchers to constitute a period socially different from their own. A full-scale research design could be made in an effort to evaluate the conditions bringing about the newer designations. Here, as in other varieties of social research, we look for similarities and differences within and between categories, searching for the relative degree of homogeneity within categories selected and comparing this with the relative degree of homogeneity between categories. A hypothesis could be formed: The progressive fragmentation of social roles into ever increasing numbers of subroles is a consequence of the need to create additional consumer markets in a market-oriented society. Or, the progressive fragmentation of roles is inversely related to the integration of the age group included within the decision-making processes of a society. I am not certain which form I would select; any selection requires a great deal of thought and preliminary testing. Other hypotheses will suggest themselves to the student.

Once the form of the hypothesis is specified, the necessary categories to serve as indicators must be specified. Unlike content analysis, which calls for rigorous coding of data and their subsequent enumeration, the categories here are not such as to permit the use of redundant measures. Once one has defined the period in which the present meaning was either unknown or undergoing transformation, the next step should be to define the *kinds* of artifacts that will constitute one's sample of the past. Magazines, newspapers, popular fiction, movies, and similar mass media are important here; but so, too, are diaries, letters, postcards, old photographs, biographies written at the time, pop songs, and the like. Do not attempt to read any present-day accounts of the period under consideration. The objective is to immerse oneself in the actual materials of that time, the primary sources, and obtain insights from these. What picture of role relationships and social stratification is presented by these sources? Do not be eager to make an immediate comparison with your own time: Remember that no matter how vital the events of your own life appear to you, subsequent generations will find our times as "corny" as we find times earlier than ours.

It is important to search for the first occurrence of a particular concept-designating word. Precisely when did *teenager* first appear? Where and how was it first used? What had happened immediately before to encourage such a usage? How was the term picked up by others? Does it still mean quite the same thing? Was it initially a term of opprobrium or a flattering term? These are the types of questions that soon become categories in one's research design. We begin to note the instances in which the term was used and those in which it was not used, and our attention is drawn to the social class of those employing the term and the manner in which it was employed. It may be that the term was first used by advertisers rather than by child counselors or educators. Incidentally, whatever happened to the term *juvenile delinquent*? Somehow that became entangled in the adolescent *vs.* teenager discussion and faded. We still have *juvenile courts* and the like, but then we still have courts of chancery, too; what survives in technical usage is something quite apart from our central problem.

Ultimately, the research design should solidify as more and more information is gathered. It is a good idea to keep notes on 3″ x 5″ file cards, alphabetically arranged by subject, rather than solely in notebooks. The use of notebooks should not be eliminated, for one needs a permanent record of ideas, lengthy passages copied from published materials, and sketches and diagrams of the relationships tentatively posed between variables. But index cards do provide the best way of filing data, including sources, that one has accumulated. The fact that they can be rearranged in order or spread out so that relationships can be examined is extremely important in this kind of research.

It is important that one have access to a good dictionary, such as the *Oxford English Dictionary,* wherein the root meanings and origins of words are specified. If one is dealing with very early

English-language books, the *Short Title Catalog* may be found useful. Items such as these and the *DNB* * are available in the reference room of any fair-sized library. The use of such reference sources is extremely important. Reference librarians are usually very helpful, no matter what one's experiences may be with the rest of the staff. They know where materials are, how to obtain them, and the lending policies of other institutions. It very often happens that the book or periodical desired is not at the library you regularly use. Very often the reference librarian can either have the book shipped to the library for you or have photocopies made of specific pages. It is extremely important, however, to know precisely what you want before you have it transferred from another library. Do not waste the librarian's time or your own on worthless fishing expeditions.

Most state libraries have a library loan service and can furnish your university or public library with copies of books they have in their stacks. In addition, if your university library has a computerized catalog system, you should learn to use it. Very often, by sitting at a terminal no more complicated than a typewriter and employing a few code words, you can "search" the stacks and journals for references to your particular research problem. Sometimes complete journal indexes, going back many years, may be searched in a matter of moments. For example, at a university in upstate New York, one can sit at a terminal in the sociology building and, by typing in a word such as *role,* obtain in moments a complete listing of the journal articles containing the word *role* in their titles; by typing in another code word, one can obtain short abstracts of each article that has been referenced. This material appears on one's own terminal, usually in typewritten form for easy study and filing. Although many students with humanistic interests are initially put off by this technological innovation and perhaps afraid of making errors in manipulating the terminal, a few minutes of experience in retrieving information in this manner will quickly dispel all fears. Some systems are set up in such a way that one has com-

* *Dictionary of National Biography.* This is a standardized abbreviation; similarly, *STC* stands for *Short Title Catalog* and *OED* for *Oxford English Dictionary.* The sociology student unfamiliar with the notations employed in historical research should consult the first pages of the journals covering his area of interest, where such abbreviations are usually listed. See also the Modern Language Association (MLA) style sheet, available at all libraries.

puter access to all the libraries within a certain geographical area. One does not need to know about computer languages to employ these systems. They are programmed in such a way that you speak to the computer by typing out your message, and the computer replies to you on your own machine. If you goof, the computer simply types out MEANING NOT CLEAR or its equivalent, asking you to rephrase your inquiry. It is very patient and will sit there all day unless you "sign off" in the manner prescribed by your facility.

Excursions into the remote past for historiographic sociological research are very demanding and require a great deal of erudition on the part of the student. However, studies of the origins of one's own community or town can be rewarding, particularly if they involve a question of sociological significance. That one's own community is directly related to the often "abstract" concepts one has learned in sociology classes may come as something of a shock. But sociology does, after all, deal with the real world, or at least it should.

Changes in the ethnic composition of the population, social stratification, distribution of life chances, and the like have all taken place within one's own town. Local historical societies and county courthouses are important sources of information for such research. The former often contain handwritten diaries, hand-drawn maps, memoirs, and artifacts of earlier periods. The county courthouses almost always contain tax records going back to the very beginning of the town's settlement, as well as probated wills and the like. There are also graveyards. If one comes from a town settled in the early English, Dutch, or Spanish days, graveyards are an important source of dates. Their location, too, can often be significant in understanding the physical layout of the early settlement. There are cemeteries for slaves, for example, throughout most of the East, predating Emancipation. The location of these cemeteries in relation to the main house of the plantation and to the white cemeteries can tell us a great deal. In the graveyard at the church in Tappan, New York, for example, favorite slaves are buried alongside their masters and mistresses. These graves date from the late seventeenth and early eighteenth centuries. A few miles south, in Norwood, New Jersey, far back in the woods (if the woods are still there!) is a slave cemetery in which no whites are buried. The cemetery is located not far from where the plantation house stood and dates from the late 1700's. Does the difference in burial customs represent a shift in the institution of slavery? Here are early Dutch settlers, in an area conquered by the English in the intervening years. Did the intrusion of English-speaking people change the attitude of the Dutch toward their slaves? We are dealing with a primary relationship, an affective bond between master and slave. Slavery on the Northern plantations was never the large-scale affair that it became in the South, and it must be presumed that the slaves were included in primary-group structures with their masters. The study of such structured relationships is one of our principal concerns in sociology.

Here, then, is an occasion for definite social research, related to broad theoretical implications such as those found in the writings of Mead and Cooley. An attempt to explore the social construction of reality among Dutch settlers of New Amsterdam when confronted with a competing, dominant reality, that of the English settlers who conquered them, may yield valuable sociological data. Of course, one needs to study more than one or two Dutch graveyards and their records to pose a solution to the problem. But it is a place to start.

Similarly, settlements of American Indians may be studied or early Jewish cemeteries or the Portuguese, Spanish, or Italian settlements. But such study, it must be remembered, should be related to one's research design and hence should deal with relevant concepts as variables.

The results of such research are usually written as straight narrative, although maps and charts of a descriptive nature should be included, if possible, for purposes of comparison. References must be carefully listed, together with the name and location of the specific documents discussed. Since one's sources are primary, usually only one copy of a document is available, and the reader must be informed where this can be found.

I will not readily forget an experience of my own in conducting research associated with the use of slaves by the Jersey Dutch. The original maps of northern New Jersey and southern New York made by General Erskine for General George Washington during the Revolution are owned by the New York Historical Society in New York City. My research had led me to consider the origin of a small town in northern New Jersey that had originally been part of a town now wholly located within the state of New York. The problems associated with state lines are numerous; the actual lines dividing two states have, in many instances, been defined only recently. I had searched in vain for maps showing some detail of the area in which my little town was located during the Revolutionary War, when it was part of the larger town to the north. When the Dutch had settled the area, state lines did not exist. The photocopies of the Erskine maps at the local historical societies had proved insufficient. I therefore traveled to New York City to examine the originals.

In most libraries containing rare documents and maps, one searches through a card file describing each item, then selects the ones desired, and presents the catalog number to the librarian, who then brings photocopies made from the originals; this is to ensure that the originals do not become badly damaged by handling. If the photocopies are not clear enough for one's purposes, the originals may sometimes be viewed in special rooms, provided that one does not take pencils, pens, or anything else that may damage the original into the room. One must also be able to justify the need to examine the original.

I had searched through the index cards with little success. There were some maps related to my problem, but the existence of a map that would show the precise geographical area of my interest, and in sufficient detail show related areas, house locations, and names as well, appeared remote. However, in searching through the cards, which are arranged in order of contingent locations of places described, I strayed from my immediate area of concern and began reading the cards associated with place names I knew; these were places remote from my little town but of marginal interest to me because of my knowledge of the state as a whole. I was puzzled on finding a card that described a map of "that part of the road running from Fort Lee to Suffran's Tavern." In my study of the maps back at the local historical society, there had been no road indicated between these two towns; there is none today. (To get from Fort Lee to Suffern one can take Route 6 west and then Route 17 north, or a variety of interconnecting roads that did not exist in the earlier days.) Moreover, by this time I had a fairly good idea where the early Revolutionary War roads lay, and I began trying to construct a mental journey between the two towns. I concluded that there was no road in the general area defined by this segment of the map collection that one could take from the fort to the tavern. Something was wrong. Either a road existed that I did not know about, or the map had been inappropriately filed. More to satisfy my curiosity than anything else, I included the call number of this map in the list I handed to the librarian.

When she brought the copies to me I skimmed through them rapidly until I came to the one purporting to show the road from the fort to the tavern. I was shocked. It was a map of my little town, showing not only the houses but the trees, the fences, the curves of the land, the swampy areas—much more than I could have hoped for. Moreover, it was the actual working map made by the surveyor as he moved along the road: It showed his line-of-sight readings to various landmarks, the compass bearings, and marginal notations on where the compass needle "deflected badly." There were even groups of calculations on the margins, where he had added or subtracted differences in angular measurements. Each little creek was indicated, each rise or fall of the ground, and each little house. And the names of homeowners were included.

The thrill of discovery more than compensated for the drudgery involved. Finding what one never suspected was there, or what had been neglected or misplaced by others so that it had remained unintentionally hidden, is the kind of reward scholars dream of. It can be yours, as it has been mine. Once experienced, it will never be forgotten. It creates a bond between researcher and research that can be created in no other way and immerses one further in the research at hand.

I had been working on the problem touched upon on page 125, the change in the idea of master-slave relations brought about by the English conquest of Dutch New Amsterdam. In the earliest graveyards of the Dutch settlers, slaves were buried alongside their masters. In graveyards subsequent to the English conquest, however, this was not the case. The problem then becomes one of determining where they were buried. Maps made for military purposes during a war such as that of the American Revolution always show the locations of houses whose inhabitants are known to be on one or the other side in the conflict. By locating the site of the plantation house and its immediate fields, and then transferring the location to a modern map, I could determine what burial grounds were associated with particular slaveholding families; most of these cemeteries still exist. I could then examine those graveyards originally located well within the boundaries of an early plantation. Once this was done it became evident that after the English conquest, Dutch farmers buried their slaves in one graveyard, and their own families in another, although both burial grounds were located on the plantation rather than in the churchyards. Consider what this may mean. They could have continued to use the church graveyard. However, there are records that show that the English settlers, who now held political power, did not bury their slaves in churchyards, and some English settlers used this same churchyard for their own families. The Dutch families could have defied the English, but this was risky. Alternatively, they could have continued to use the churchyard for their own kin, and buried the slaves elsewhere, perhaps on their plantations. This would have placed them on the best terms with the English, but would have broken the perceived paternal bond between themselves and their slaves. The choice they settled upon, that of burying their kin and their slaves on their own land, although in separate burial grounds, solved the problem for them.

Master and slave remained bound together on the very soil that had bound them together in life. True, they "slept separately," but they had done so in life as well. Moreover, the separate burial grounds would not be offensive to the English; had the Dutch transferred their churchyard custom to their own ground, then it would be plainly evident to the conquerors that the English view of the slave-master relationship was being repudiated by the Dutch. The arrangement, then, seems to represent the best compromise between conflicting tensions within the Dutch community brought about by English domination.

Rituals associated with birth and death are jealously maintained by communal groups, and the mixing of two cultures presents threats to the solidarity of the community if they touch upon such sacred customs. The Dutch action is an example of accommodation to an alien culture for the purposes of maintaining group solidarity and hence group identity. Because it involves structured relationships between two social classes within the community—between masters and slaves—it is of sociological importance. Since the question we are always asking is "How is society possible?" the study of historical transitions may help to provide an answer. Part of this answer is that society is possible if relationships between groups are structured in ways that provide reciprocity between these groups.

Anything that threatens the set of reciprocal relationships between groups threatens the society. In the face of such threats the structure must be flexible enough to permit accommodation without breaking the structural bond. In the case of the Jersey Dutch a solution was found that maintained the paternal bond between master and slave in the face of a competing view of the relationship between master and slave that threatened its disruption. The English view of slavery that posed the threat saw the slave as less than human. The slave trade in America was the product of English Puritan contempt for those not "elected" by God to perform His work, and the black African fell into this category. It is interesting that such accommodation by the Dutch enabled them to maintain their communal identity in the face of the mercantilism and aggressive business practices of the English Puritans.

Although both groups in America came out of the same Protestant reformist movement, and were able to persist side by side in relative harmony for more than a hundred years, the policy of accommodation was entirely one-sided. Little effort was made by the English conquerors to accommodate themselves to the Dutch settlers. In the absence of political power, such a policy would have been disastrous. But with political power on their side, the English were able to resist any threats posed by the earlier Dutch. Their own internal structuring was secure, and, however rigid the bonds, political power ensured their maintenance. The policy of accommodation by the Dutch never completely destroyed their identity. The Vanderbilts, Roosevelts, and other families of the early Dutch community learned much from the English, and by adopting their business practices were able to persist and succeed in the very areas that distinguished the Puritan ethic. If the Dutch had abandoned their view of the relationship between master and slave and had adopted the English view, they probably would have been absorbed into the English community and their own identity would have disappeared.

It is such considerations as these that interest the sociologist engaged in historical studies. He is not interested in history as history: He is interested in the structures that make history possible. His purposes are different from those of the historian. Both seek to understand the patterns in history and both employ many of the same methods. The historian, however, begins by taking the existence of society for granted and looks for the unique events within society. The sociologist does not take the existence of society for granted. For him, as for Simmel, the very fact that societies can exist is the problem to be explained.

SUGGESTED READINGS

Erikson, Kai T., *Wayward Puritans* (New York: Wiley, 1966).

Glass, D. V., and D. E. C. Wrigley (eds.), *Population in History* (London: Arnold, 1965).

Lazarsfeld, Paul F., *Historical Analysis* (Boston: Allyn & Bacon, 1972).

Von Martin, Alfred, *The Sociology of the Renaissance* (New York: Harper & Row, 1963).

Weber, Max, *The City* (New York: Free Press, 1966).

Wrigley, E. A. (ed.), *An Introduction to English Historical Demography* (New York: Basic Books, 1966).

Zito, George V., "A Note on the Population of 17th Century London," *Demography*, 9 (August, 1972).

# 6

# *Taxonomies and Theories Research*

BECAUSE OF THE DIVERSITY of sociological research methods it may seem as if there are few, if any, underlying assumptions common to all. But as we have seen, *the basic analytical process is the same no matter what technique is employed to obtain the data.* Whether one's analytical techniques are quantitative or not, the analytical process is the same. Quantitative methods and qualitative methods consider the data in the same way at the level of conceptualization. This is particularly true since the basic relationship we have been discussing,

$$X \longrightarrow Y$$

is not only the form of the hypothesis but the form of the basic *logical proposition.* It attempts to show a relationship between concepts by linking two concepts together.

*A proposition links two concepts in a relationship. A set of propositions linked together is a theory.*

We can see now why it is impossible to separate *theory* and *method.* Historical researcher, participant observer, survey analyst, content analyst—all look for some X and some Y, whether they start with a hypothesis already formed and attempt to reject it or allow the hypothesis to develop as a result of their critical observations, with or without operational definitions. Most research begins with theoretical propositions drawn from the major theorists, since such theorists have specified many sets of relationships (that is, many sets of propositions) in their theories. Now we can begin to understand why, as I mentioned earlier, a great deal of the published research examines the work of the major social theorists. Such research attempts to test the theorists' asserted relationships between concepts by applying them to observable action in the real world. It attempts to test what has been affirmed against empirical experience.

Because quantitative and nonquantitative methods alike are forced to employ logical propositions and theories, it is apparent that the latter must have *logical internal consistency*. For example, if we are asserting,

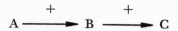

then we cannot, at the same time, assert,

$$A \xrightarrow{\ +\ } B \xrightarrow{\ +\ } C$$
$$\text{\small$-$}$$

since if A has a positive relationship to B, and B a positive relationship to C, then the relationship between A and C must also be positive and cannot be negative. Of course, such a set of conflicting, internally inconsistent relationships could be derived from participant observation; that is, we may find, as a result of our field work, that contradictory sets of beliefs are held by a person or group. But note that we could never make such a determination unless what *we* were doing in analyzing the observed beliefs was logically consistent. Indeed, one form of sociological research investigates *axiomatic theory*—that is, by isolating the set of propositions in a theory, determines their internal consistency. We may do this by determining the basic axioms of a theorist, writing his assertions in the form of propositions, and arranging these propositions in the order demanded by the propositions themselves, whether or not the theorist has placed them in that order:

1(a) The greater the number of people in a population, the greater the division of labor.

 (b) The greater the division of labor, the lower the social integration.

 (c) The lower the social integration, the greater the alienation.

2(a) The greater the division of labor, the greater the urbanization.

 (b) The less the division of labor, the less the urbanization.

 (c) The less the division of labor, the greater the family ties.

 (d) The greater the family ties, the less the alienation.

From 1(a) to 2(d) it follows that:

$H_0$  The greater the numbers in the population, the greater the alienation

  since a corollary to (2c) must be:

 (2c) (c) The greater the division of labor, the less the family ties

  and the corollary to ( 2d ) must be:

 (2d) (c) The less the family ties, the greater the alienation.

The derived hypothesis $H_0$, as well as the two derived corollaries, is seen to be consistent with (1a) through (1c), which specify growing alienation with growing numbers in the population and a subsequent (2c) growth of alienation with the weakening of family ties. Thus the theory is shown to be one of high internal consistency.

Whether it has any correspondence to what occurs in the real world, however, is another matter entirely. Reason and logic dictate what *should* take place; whether this *does* take place can be answered only by attempting to observe what takes place. In other words, experience and logic may be at odds here, as they frequently are. Indeed, this is perhaps one of the key areas of sociological exploration.

Because of the possible disparities between experience and logic, it is crucial to keep the observer and the observed distinctly separated in one's thinking. Although one may be in search of those taken-for-granted, yet illogical, aspects of everyday existence, his own logical premises must be secure *in order to observe what he has elected to observe.* His internal standard must be logical. In discovering the illogical or irrational, he must be prepared to deal with the problem posed in terms of its *consequences* in the phenomenon being studied. In defining phenomena and the concepts relating to them, two possible approaches suggest themselves.

## DEFINITIONS

In Chapter 1, I spoke of *operationalization,* the process of making operational definitions. Let us go back a step and place this whole matter on a firmer footing.

Definitions are of two kinds. A definition may be made in terms of words or in terms of properties, actions, and attributes that can be measured, and which one understands to represent the concept defined. The first form of definition, that employing words, is called a constitutive definition.

*A constitutive definition defines a concept (word) in terms of other concepts (words).* If I define a norm as an expectation of behavior, I am defining the word *norm* by two other words, *expectation* and *behavior.* There are concepts denoted by each of these three words; hence, I am defining a concept by two other concepts.

*An operational definition defines a concept (word) in terms of indicators of that concept (word).* If I define *status* as a position in a structure, I am making a constitutive definition, of the same kind as I made in defining *norm.* However, I could define status in terms of ranking on three indicators: a scale of income, another of education, and a third of occupation. I could specify these scales and specify also whether they are to be determined on the basis of the individual's true attainments or from the viewpoint of others in the community. Here I would be providing an operationalization of the concept *status.* I would be saying that an individual's status in a community (that is, his position in a structure) may be determined from indicators that my theoretical perspective dictates measure *status.*

Very few theories are founded entirely upon operationalized definitions, and very few examples of research can be cited in which each concept employed in the research design ends up in measurable form and is supplied with suitable indicators. More

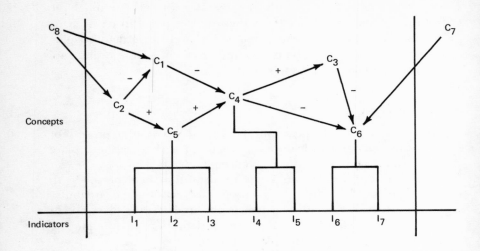

Figure 6-1. A set of constitutive definitions relating concepts into a theory of propositions, with some indicators supplied to concepts at lower levels of abstraction.

often than not, research takes the form shown in Figure 6–1. In this figure, all concepts are shown as C's, all indicators as I's. The theoretical propositions are readily recognized: A positive relationship is stated between concepts $C_2$ and $C_5$, linking them into a proposition, and $C_5$ and $C_4$ have a similar positive relationship. Hence, the theory states that as $C_2$ increases, $C_5$ will increase and then $C_4$; also, as $C_2$ increases, $C_1$ should *decrease,* since a negative relationship is asserted between $C_2$ and $C_1$. A negative relationship is also posited between $C_1$ and $C_4$, so that as $C_1$ decreases, $C_4$ should *increase.* Nothing inconsistent here.

Note that the indicators are at the lowest level of abstraction and are supplied to only three concepts; the hypothesis being tested here is the relationship between $C_5$ and $C_6$, where $C_5$ is the *independent variable,* X, and $C_6$ the *dependent variable,* Y. $C_4$ is an *intervening variable.* Of the variables shown, $C_5$ and $C_6$ are at the lowest level of abstraction; the theory is here being tested by operationalizing the two concepts at the lowest level of abstraction, since these are the most accessible to empirical tests (being less abstract than the others). Although $C_4$ is at a higher level of abstraction than $C_5$ or $C_6$, the researcher feels obliged to test it, since he suspects its function as an intervening variable; it is evident that increasing $C_5$ should show a decrease in $C_6$, because the intervening variable is shown with a negative link to the dependent variable.

$C_1$ and $C_3$ are at high levels of abstraction and are less amenable to direct testing. They have been defined in terms of the other concepts, employing constitutive definitions. This is also true of $C_8$ and $C_7$, which are at very high levels of abstraction, and which the theory represented here sees as *exogenous variables*—that is, variables external to the system of concepts under consideration, although they make some contribution to the final result. In the contingency tables that could result from research of this kind, some of the cases that do not fit the pattern of the resulting diagonals could possibly be attributed to these exogenous variables. In other words, in precision research we must somehow explain why deviant cases occur in our results. *Deviant-case analysis* attempts to find common denominators of the deviant cases, what they have in common that is different from those cases that *do* fall on the diagonal of the table.

Before we leave Figure 6–1, one or two other points should be made. The variables included *within* the research design (that is, those other than $C_8$ and $C_7$) are referred to as *endogenous variables*. I might also mention that the extreme operational viewpoint referred to earlier would insist that only $I_1, \ldots I_7$ are *real*.

## TAXONOMIES

Definitions provide a useful bridge to the construction of *taxonomies*, or *typologies*, as they are also called. The *definitional taxonomy* is relatively easy to construct from constitutive definitions and theoretical propositions. On page 135 I mentioned that *status* might be defined as a *position* in a *structure*. Note that I defined a relatively abstract concept, *status,* by employing two concepts (*position* and *structure*) at lower levels of abstraction than status. This is a general rule in supplying scientific definitions. The so-called Oxford Rule attempted to disentangle philosophy from the confusion of language. The rule states quite simply that in defining any word we should employ words more concrete in reference than the original word. This means defining a concept by employing concepts that are at lower levels of abstraction. If we look back at Figure 6–1, this means it is permissible to define $C_8$ in terms of $C_2$ and $C_1$, or $C_3$ in terms of $C_4$ and $C_6$, but it is not permissible to define $C_4$ in terms of $C_1$ and $C_3$. If $C_4$ is to be defined, it must be in terms of $C_5$ and $C_6$.

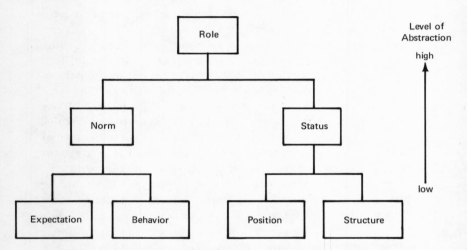

**Figure 6-2. Definitional taxonomy of some sociological concepts.**

Figure 6–2 employs the definition of *status* together with the definitions of *norm* and *role,* and these concepts are arranged in a *taxonomy,* or classification diagram.

The figure offers the following definitions:

A *norm* is an *expectation* of *behavior.*
A *status* is a *position* in a *structure.*
A *role* is a *norm* of a *status.*

The concepts *expectation, behavior, position,* and *structure* are shown to be all at about the same level of abstraction, although it might be argued that *expectation* is more abstract than the other three. It is, however, less abstract than *norm*, which it is being used to define. The same is true for *position* and *structure*: Both are less abstract concepts than *status*. At the highest level in this taxonomy is *role*: It is the most abstract and most difficult to define. Some sociologists may even quarrel with its definition here as a norm associated with a status. If we read the definition implied by the taxonomy, *a role is an expectation of behavior associated with one's position in a structure*, or *a role is a norm of a status*, or *a role is a norm associated with a status*.

In constructing such taxonomies, we arrange our categories in hierarchical order according to an underlying dimension. Here the dimension is the *level of abstraction*. But other dimensions may be employed, depending upon one's research problem. The most familiar *hierarchical taxonomy* is the bureaucratic structure of a corporation or government, which shows the distribution of authority as one climbs the ladder. The president is at the top, the vice-presidents beneath him, various executives beneath them, and so forth. Here the dimension is the *level of authority* vested in the offices. Another familiar hierarchical taxonomy is the biological schema, which classifies organisms as *kingdom, phylum, species,* and the like. Just as in the case of Figure 6–2, each step higher includes those entries beneath it.

There are some taxonomies that are "nonhierarchical," but they are simply two-level affairs and are probably not taxonomies in a true sense. Seeman's alienation paradigm,* mentioned in Chapter 3, can serve as one example. Here we would place *alienation* at the top and the other terms, such as *normlessness, powerlessness,* and so on, on another, lower level.

## REIFICATION AND INFINITE REGRESS

Taxonomic and theory research employing axiomatic analysis are *heuristic* in nature; that is, they help us to *discover* new properties or relationships of which we are initially unaware. Since most of the work we perform at first in conducting such research is at the nonempirical level, it is necessary to provide constant logical checks on our procedures. The fallacies intro-

---

* A *paradigm* is a conceptual model.

duced in Chapters 1 and 2, such as the *ecological fallacy, reductionism*, and the like, must be kept constantly in mind. Categories must be kept mutually exclusive and exhaustive. Internal logical consistency must be evident. The possibility that intervening variables may play a part in the relationship cannot be ignored.

However, the extent to which intervening variables are considered poses an interesting problem. Suppose that one is considering the relationship between working mothers and delinquent sons. One might hypothesize that juvenile delinquency is more frequent in families where the mother works outside the home and is therefore absent the greater part of the day, or some version of this once popular supposition about the causes of juvenile delinquency. Suppose that one has phrased the problem in terms of the dichotomy of *instrumental vs. emotive-expressive* roles. The hypothesis may be in the form:

The greater the emotive-expressive activity of the mother, the lower the performance of deviant activity of the son.

Here a negative relationship is specified, as follows:

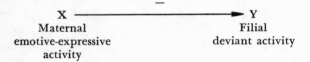

If one were to conduct empirical research on this hypothesis, the probability of finding a perfect relationship in the resulting contingency table would be very slim. Many cases will be found of high X but low Y, and of low X and high Y, but many also (though fewer) of high X and high Y, and of low X and low Y. In other words, the four-celled contingency table may disclose a diagonal in the predicted direction, but there will be many cases falling into the other two cells as well. How are we to account for the other cases?

Examining our data, we may suspect that the socio-economic status of the mother has an effect. It may be that deviant behavior in sons is more prevalent where the mother is economically insecure or drawn from a lower-class background. Further examination of the data may show that this is not completely true, but that such families are most often living in depressed neighborhoods. It may be that the following condition prevails:

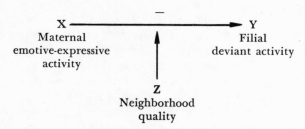

Figure 6–3. *Neighborhood quality* as a conditional variable.

Figure 6–3 suggests that neighborhood quality acts as a conditional variable: If the maternal emotive-expressive activity is high and the neighborhood quality is high, then filial deviance is low; but if the maternal expressive activity is high and the neighborhood quality is low, then filial deviance is high. If we could explain all, or almost all, of the cases falling into the other cells of the contingency table by such a paradigm, we would be satisfied in our belief that neighborhood quality served as a conditional variable in the hypothesized relationship between maternal emotive-expressive activity and filial deviant activity.

But suppose that we had sought the explanation of our other cells along another dimension. Suppose that we had data on the families and knew how many siblings each son in our sample had, their sex, age, and miscellaneous other characteristics. We might be tempted to suppose that the number of children present in the household served as an intervening variable, that the more children the mother had, the greater the probability of deviant activity on the part of her sons. We might arrive at a hypothesized relationship such as that of Figure 6–4.

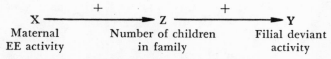

Figure 6–4. *Number of children* as an intervening variable.

Here we are asserting two things: (1) that women who engage in a great deal of emotive-expressive activity have a large number of children and (2) that the large number of children in the family serves as the source of deviant activity on the part of the sons. The first part of the relationship is positive; the second is also positive. All well and good, it might be objected, but what is the role played by the quality of the neighborhood? This may still act as a conditional variable, but it could be argued that families with a great number of children probably stand a greater chance of living in a low-quality neighborhood, on the basis of cost alone. Since what is being argued is that a fixed income level forces large families to live in less desirable residential areas than they might otherwise choose, *neighborhood quality* is being seen as an intervening variable, a consequence of family economic level. Hence, the hypothesis is taking the form of Figure 6–5. Here we are stating that the

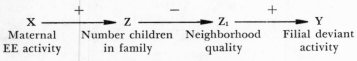

Figure 6–5.   Two intervening variables.

greater the mother's emotive-expressive activity, the greater the number of children she will have, and the greater the number of children, the lower the quality of neighborhood in which the family can afford to live, and therefore the greater the likelihood of the sons' deviance. However, the hypothesis of Figure 6–5 seems to become less satisfying the more we work on it. Perhaps the Z specified is not specific enough. Does it not make a difference if the children are all sons in large families, particularly if the neighborhood quality is low? Perhaps we should include another variable, $Z_2$, *sex of siblings,* between Z and $Z_1$. But would this be correct? It implies that families with sons only stand a greater chance of choosing a low-quality neighborhood than families with daughters only. That may strike one as not improbable, in which case we now have three intervening variables. And on and on we go, adding an infinite number of intervening variables between our principal two.

It soon comes as no great surprise that we could continue this process forever and still not be completely satisfied. We are trapped in a logical predicament. In a desperate attempt to extricate ourselves, we look at our first variable, X. Why are some mothers performing more emotive-expressive activity than others? Possibly because of the available time at their disposal. But why does the time vary? Possibly because some have to work outside the home and others do not. Why must some work and others not? Possibly because those in the first group are widowed, have husbands who earn insufficient money to support the family, or simply prefer to work. Why do some prefer to work under any condition, some husbands earn less than others, and some women raise families as widows? This "Why, Daddy?" attitude, so familiar in the questions of very young children, is part and parcel of the same problem that confronted us when we began supplying intervening variables and antecedent variables to our basic hypothesis. There can be no end to such a series of questions; we can continually descend to lower and lower orders of questioning, higher and higher levels of abstraction, or simply continue to ask *why* without ever reaching a point of logical termination. This is the problem of *infinite regress*. It makes itself particularly evident when we are caught in the trap of assuming *causality* rather than searching for *correlation*. It is sufficient to show that a particular class of phenomena is *associated* with another class of phenomena without venturing too far into the causal dimension. The student may find this unsatisfactory, but at this stage of our knowledge we cannot do very much more than this. Indeed, it may be logically impossible *ever* to do more than this, at least in the social sciences. At some point in logical analysis one must be satisfied with the adequacy of the categories he is employing and venture no further. This precludes our ever making any *absolutely* true statement. The problem of causal inference, first defined by David Hume (1711–76), is a profound one.

The problem of infinite regress is particularly troublesome in taxonomic and axiomatic research, where one is operating wholly on the conceptual level. There are usually so many possible contingencies that must be considered. Here, as in empirical research, the most one can do is attempt to identify the *major categories* and show their relations, one to another. One may split hairs *ad infinitum* without making substantial progress or explaining anything more than what was explained initially. Indeed, one may end by explaining less, since the confusion introduced by a large number of variables that cannot be handled mentally at one time can be considerable. Simplicity and conceptual clarity are demanded by good research.

Another problem that may arise is usually referred to as *reification*, the making of a "thing" from a nonthing, such as a process or abstraction. Things that are not real may be real in their consequences if they are believed to be real, as W. I. Thomas (1863–1947) pointed out. But this does not mean that all things have the same *kind* of existence; some things exist in space and time, some exist at discrete locations, but others exist only diffusely, or as ideas, mental images, and the like, as *properties* of other things. A color, for example, is not a thing but a property of a thing. Is justice a thing? Are virtue, love, honor things? Probably not. This does not mean that we must dismiss them as irrelevant; it does mean, however, that we cannot treat them as objects when we are comparing objects, any more than we can treat color as an object. We must be careful to distinguish properties and processes from objects and to apply only the appropriate treatment to each.

A *metaphor* is a kind of analogy. We do a great deal of our speaking and thinking in terms of metaphorical meanings: We speak of individual *actors*, who perform *roles*, but we do not really mean to suggest that the *dramatistic metaphor* we are employing is entirely accurate; what we mean is that the socialized individual has properties *like those of an actor* and performs some patterned activities much as an actor does. To go beyond metaphorical usage is difficult, but some efforts in sociology at present are advancing in that direction.

In attempting to understand social phenomena with which one has only marginal familiarity, it is necessary to recheck one's own biases continually. We saw this to be true in participant observation; it is true in any sociological research. Since many sociologists have been drawn from predominantly middle-class backgrounds (up to this present generation only middle-class parents could afford an extended university education for their children), a great deal of traditional sociology reveals a middle-class bias. This is true of European as well as American sociology. It is only very recently that "ethnics" have had a chance to make contributions to our knowledge of society and social processes. The middle-class researcher will find much reinforcement of his biases from his colleagues and from the academic community generally. That which is "taken for granted" by any community, including a community of scholars, is likely to be predicated upon shared traditional beliefs concerning what is "real" and what is not.

A "sociology of sociology" has come into existence, which challenges many of the taken-for-granted assumptions and attempts to evaluate the direction of research and the research findings themselves in terms of the class background of the researcher. Such concerns should not be dismissed lightly. Any discipline, particularly one that deals with human beings, must continually question its procedures and findings. The results of our research can be only as value-free as we ourselves are, and that is usually not very much. The student researcher as well as the more advanced professional must exercise a great deal of caution in order to avoid the commission of errors that can have consequences in the lives of people other than himself. He must also be wary of implications in his research findings that may have class biases or logical flaws. A certain ethical and moral responsibility is involved in research activity, and the mere fact that one is "only a student" does not relieve him of responsibility. What appears to be incontestably true in our taxonomic or axiomatic operations, or as a result of a necessarily limited amount of statistical sampling, may not be true from public definitions of the situation. Hence, communicating one's findings to other sociologists is one thing, and communicating with the public respecting such findings is another. The levels of responsibility differ, but responsibility is involved in both instances. The safest procedure is to re-examine one's assumptions continually as one proceeds in the investigation and, when it is completed, to realize that any findings are wholly tentative.

Logical consistency is extremely important in any research. So is ethical and moral responsibility.

SUGGESTED READINGS

Alker, Hayward R., "A Typology of Ecological Fallacies," in Mattei Dogan and Stern Rokkan (eds.), *Quantitative Ecological Analysis in Social Sciences* (Cambridge: University of Massachusetts Press, 1969).

Bailey, Kenneth D., "Monothetic and Polythetic Typologies and Their Relation to Conceptualization, Measurement and Scaling," *American Sociological Review* 38 (February, 1973).

Stinchecomb, A. L., *Constructing Social Theories* (New York: Harcourt Brace & World, 1968).

# 7

# *Property Space and Correlation*

ONE OF THE PRINCIPAL USES of taxonomies (or typologies) is in the *reduction of property space*. Paul Lazarsfeld introduced this terminology to describe an important function performed by social research. To understand what this means, let us go back to Chapter 3 and reconsider some of the results of our survey-research example, particularly Figures 3–1 through 3–5, which present the resulting contingency tables.

It will be remembered that the original hypothesis was that socialization processes in the form of peer-group pressures were more effective with freshmen than with seniors. By *controlling* for place of residence (Figure 3–2), we saw that this did not hold, and the results suggested other variables, which we proceeded to control for in our results. Our final contingency table was the 16-cell Figure 3–5, in which we control for place of origin (local/out of state) and place of residence (dormitory/off-campus) of the seniors and freshmen we interviewed. We noticed that when we controlled to this extent we began to find empty (or *null*) cells in our table. Does this tell us something?

We have already noted the possibility that whenever we control for a great number of sources of variation and our sample is small ($n = 60$ in the case of the Chapter 3 example), we begin to get cells with smaller sums in them. We expect this by simple division: 16 into 60 is smaller than 8 into 60, which is smaller than 4 into 60. But if the fall-off rate is greater in some cells than in others, it must be true that these cells are explaining less of the variation in the dependent variable. As a matter of fact, the results of Figure 3–5 (which shows only one way the data may have turned out, you will remember) would be very discouraging if we actually found them.

Remembering the row-column system of designation introduced in Chapter 1 (p. 11), let us designate the cells (C) of Figure 3–5 accordingly. The uppermost and left cell is therefore $C_{11}$, and the bottommost and right cell is $C_{82}$.* If we examine Figure 3–5, we see that the central portion includes relatively few cases. Of the eight cells, $C_{31}, \ldots C_{62}$, four are null (cells $C_{41, \; 42}$, $_{52, \; 62}$) and four others include a total of only five cases ($C_{31} = 2$, $C_{32} = 1$, $C_{51} = 1$, $C_{61} = 1$). This means that these eight combinations do not account for much variation; four of them account for none at all, and the other four for very little. Apparently we are not finding so many combinations as we logically know are possible. If our survey is really representative, there is a possibility that these particular cells represent categories dictated by logic but not found in sufficiently large numbers in actual experience to be worth considering in terms of nomothetic principles. Perhaps we can collapse our 16-cell table into a table with fewer cells.

One way to collapse the table is simply to eliminate the central eight cells that do not show much, discarding the five cases they contain. To do this we would have to eliminate either variable W or variable Z, or combine them into one variable. Thus one category would be *local students living in dormitories* and another *out-of-state students living off campus*. This yields the contingency table shown in Figure 7–1; the $n = 55$, rather than 60, since we have thrown away the five cases from the center of the table. This is a reduction of property space, since the distinction between variables W and Z was unproductive.†

---

* There are eight rows in the table, and the first digit assigns the row, the second digit the column; therefore $C_{82}$ is the cell in the eighth row and the second column, that cell containing the number 20; similarly, cell $C_{11}$ contains the number 20, $C_{12}$ the number 0, $C_{21} = 8$, $C_{22} = 2$, and so forth.

† We have reduced the property space by reducing the number of cells necessary to explain most of the data; instead of three independent variables (X, W, Z), we now have two (V, Z).

However, there is a further reduction of property space possible that has dire consequences for any research that turns up results such as those of Figure 3–5. Examining Figure 3–5, we discover, by inspecting the marginals, that the "in" column totals 33, the "$\overline{\text{in}}$" column 27. Examining the row marginals, we notice that the first four rows sum to 33, the next four to 27. Thus we have the same marginal sums in rows and columns. This can mean only that virtually all the variation we find in our dependent variable is explained by only one of the three independent variables. In the present case, because of the way our contingency table is arranged, it is very easy to identify that variable, since it is the only one common to all four rows: variable W, *place of origin*. Retaining all our cases ($n = 60$), we see that we can reduce the property space to a four-celled contingency table very quickly.

| V | X | Y in | Y $\overline{\text{in}}$ | |
|---|---|---|---|---|
| Local students living in dorms | freshmen | 20 | 0 | 20 |
| | seniors | 8 | 2 | 10 |
| Out-of-state students living off campus | freshmen | 0 | 4 | 4 |
| | seniors | 1 | 20 | 21 |
| | | 29 | 26 | 55 |

n = 55

**Figure 7-1. A reduction of property space by eliminating cells containing few cases.**

Thus, if our data analysis turned up the results of Figure 3–5, we would be disappointed indeed. It tells us nothing about our original hypothesis regarding socialization processes of freshmen *vs.* seniors, nothing about dormitory *vs.* off-campus living. It tells us what we knew all along, that some fads are "in" on a local basis; most out-of-state students are not with it because it is a local phenomenon. If we try some deviant-case analysis, we find that the three cases in $C_{21}$ of Figure 7–2 include a freshman living in a dormitory, a senior living in a dormitory, and a senior living off campus; $C_{12}$ contains two seniors living in a dorm and one off-campus freshman. The small difference is primarily accountable to seniors living in dorms, and in the

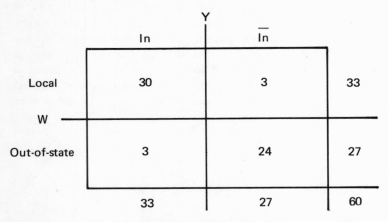

Figure 7-2. Reduction of property space identifying the independent variable explaining most of the variation in Y.

wrong direction, since two of them are not *in* and the other is from out of state.

What Figure 7–2 shows is that *place of origin* is the X in

$$X \longrightarrow Y$$

and not *class year* dichotomized as freshman/senior. Almost all of the variation in our dependent variable is explained by whether or not the student comes from the local area.

The reduction of property space is seldom so destructive to our research results. What it does most fruitfully is disclose combinations that we might suppose should exist, but which our findings show us do not, or exist in such small numbers that they are not significant. Very often a judicious application of reduction will disclose a new concept, not previously suspected.

In our discussion of scaling (pp. 74–82), we found an empty

cell in Fig. 3–8c and a Guttman scale resulting. This, too, is a reduction of property space, yielding a unidimensional scale of drug usage.

## CORRELATION AND REGRESSION

With the arsenal of research tools the student now has at his disposal, he is ready for an attack on a variety of fronts. He is equipped not only to perform a variety of research investigations but to evaluate the results of others and perhaps improve upon them. In examining the results of others, he may have occasion to see how a reduction of property space is possible where the original researcher did not. He may spot a lack of internal consistency. He may be able to read implications in the data that the researcher missed.

As he begins to examine the results of others, he will find references to *measures of association, correlation coefficients,* and *regression coefficients.* Although it is not my purpose in this text to stress quantitative measures unduly or to teach statistical techniques, it is important that all sociology students understand what the frequently employed quantitative measures mean at the level of conceptualization, whether or not they are interested in performing such computations as part of their own data analysis.

Earlier quantitative techniques in the social sciences laid much stress on *tests of statistical significance.* As noted in Chapter 4, such tests purport to show the *probability* that the results one has obtained are not produced by chance alone. Such probability may be computed and is usually shown at some significance level at the bottom of the contingency table. A notation such as "$p = .001$" or "$pr = .001$" means that the probability that the relationship disclosed is purely accidental is one in a thousand. Although many tests of statistical significance are still performed and in many cases have meaningful interpretations, attention has recently turned to *measures of association.* A measure of association is an index of the strength of the disclosed relationship. Most measures of association run from 0 (no relationship) to 1 (perfect relationship). We discussed the difference between *weak* and *strong* relationships in Chapter 2. A *strong* relationship is one lying close to 1 in association; a

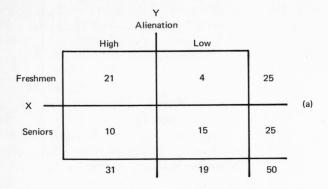

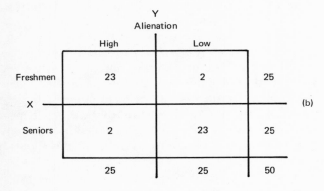

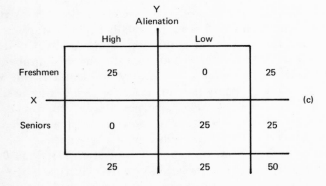

Figure 7-3. Weak, strong, and perfect inverse relationships.

*weak* relationship lies closer to 0. The strength of a relationship usually tells us more at the level of meaning than a test of statistical significance. It shows us how much of the variation in the dependent variable is associated with variation in the independent variable(s).

In Chapter 3, in discussing survey research, we proposed a scale of alienation and applied it to 25 seniors and 25 freshmen. Figure 3–6 is a contingency table of possible results. This table and some variations that could have been obtained are shown in Figure 7–3.

Figure 7–3a is identical with Figure 3–6. Although an inverse relationship is disclosed, it is not very strong, since only three-fifths of the seniors scored low on alienation, while two-fifths scored high. Figure 7–3b discloses a *stronger* relationship than that of Figure 7–3a. Here 23 of the 25 seniors (or 23/25) scored low on alienation, and hence only 2/25 scored high. Figure 2–3c shows a perfect relationship: 25/25 of seniors scored low, and 25/25 of freshmen scored high. No freshman scored low and no senior scored high. A measure of association would yield a score of 1 for Figure 7–3c and something less than 1 but greater than 0 for Figure 7–3b; for Figure 7–3a it would yield something closer to 0 than it did for Figure 7–3b. There are many different measures of association, applicable to different scales; many go by the name of the Greek letter used to designate them, such as phi for the Greek letter $\phi$; others use Roman letters, such as $Q$ or $r$.

Figure 3–6 was based upon the scores obtained by the 50 sampled students. It will be recalled that each student sampled could obtain a score from 0 to 9 on an *alienation scale*. For the sake of simplicity, we decided to dichotomize the scores into *high* and *low:* An individual obtaining a score from 0 to 4 was placed in a *low* alienation cell; one obtaining a score from 5 to 9 was placed in a *high* alienation cell. Which cell they were placed in was, of course, also contingent upon whether they were freshmen or seniors. In thus dichotomizing the dependent variable we were throwing away some of the variation in our alienation scores. Although the scores ran from 0 to 9 and therefore include ten possible values, by making them either *high* or *low* we reduced them to two values. Since our *alienation scale* is not very good to begin with—there being several different possible ways in which two individuals could obtain the same score, although they might differ markedly in what we mean by alienation—it was a sound procedure to dichotomize the results. It makes little sense to apply a highly sensitive indicator to a gross phenomenon, and the phenomenon here is indeed gross. The very fact that we obtained a weak relationship shows that our scale is not very well suited to the phenomenon we are attempting to measure. A highly accurate scale applied to very well-defined phenomena might yield the results shown in Figure 7–3c, but we probably cannot expect this kind of accuracy in social science. There are many reasons for this, including not only the variability of any property across units of analysis (in this case, individuals) but the imprecision in providing operational definitions for concepts that have no precise meanings but include a number of connotative associations.

Suppose, however, that our instrument was capable of giving us greater precision, that it could really measure small differences in alienation among and between our units of analysis. In that case, we would probably not want to throw away so much of the information our tests had disclosed. Or perhaps we are uncertain about the relative accuracy of our scale and feel that it might be best to present all the data without dichotomizing or otherwise grouping and allow the reader to make up his own mind about the accuracy of the tests used to measure the concept. One way to present the data, and gain increased understanding for ourselves as well as anyone else who wishes to analyze our results, is to employ an X-Y coordinate system in the abbreviated form shown in Figure 7–4, where each figure corresponds to the contingency tables of the previous figure.

Here we have plotted X against Y, the independent variable against the dependent variable. The vertical *ordinate* is our alienation scale, running from 0 to 9; we have indicated the *cut-off* or *break point* at 4.5, corresponding to our *low* and *high* scores. On the X axis we have only two points, *freshmen* and *seniors*. In Figure 7–4a, the 25 freshmen scores are indicated together with the 25 senior scores. We have made a mark corresponding to each individual opposite the score he obtained. As in our contingency table, 21 freshmen obtained a high score and 4 a low score, while 10 seniors obtained a high score and 15 a low score. Seeing the scores plotted this way gives us a better grasp

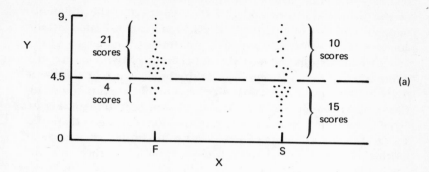

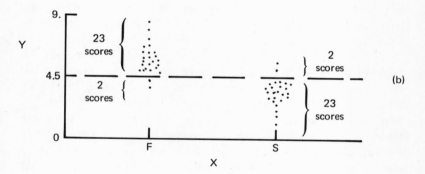

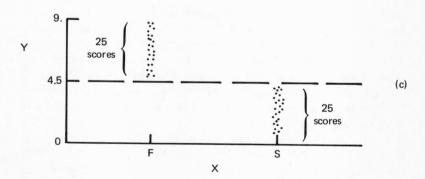

Figure 7-4. Results presented on Cartesian (X,Y) coordinates.

of the distribution *within* the high and low categories for each of the two groups. We notice, for example, that the difference *between* the two groups is even less than that indicated by the corresponding contingency table, since most of the *low* alienation scores of the seniors are near the upper limit of the *low* category, while most of the *high* scores of the freshmen are near the lower limit of the *high* category. We could not obtain this much information from Figure 3–6, so that the presentation of Figure 7–4a is retaining more of the information obtained than did Figure 3–6. As a matter of fact, Figure 3–6, although it showed us that the relationship was a weak one, did not show us how weak it really was. Obviously, if most of the *high* freshmen scores clustered near the upper limit of the *high* category, and most of the *low* senior scores clustered near the lower limit of the *low* category, the relationship between X and Y would be stronger than that disclosed in the first case. Both cases, however, yield the same cell totals.

Figure 7–4b is a plot of the table shown in Figure 7–3b. A stronger relationship is shown here than in Figure 7–4a. In addition, even if the two *high* senior cases were closer to the upper limit of the *high* category, the relationship would still be stronger than that shown in Figure 7–4a. Figure 7–4c, which plots the table of Figure 7–3c, shows a spread within the scores of the freshman category that is about the same as the spread within the senior category. This is a perfect relationship, since each category is falling into its own space: There is no overlapping of the two sets of scores; our instrument is discriminating very well. But this figure raises another problem. How *perfect* is *perfect*? Obviously our results in Figure 7–4c could take a variety of forms, some of which are shown in Figure 7–5.

Without having any overlap between *high* and *low* scores, we could obtain, from similar but not identical groups of seniors and freshmen, the results shown in each of the figures *a* through *c*. Suppose we compute the *average* or *mean* score obtained for each one of these groups. Since what we are averaging is the Y scores, let us designate this mean score by $\overline{Y}$ for each group of students. Freshmen in Figure 7–4a had a mean score of 8, seniors of 2. We obtain these means by simply adding all the freshmen scores in Figure 7–4a and dividing by 25, the number of individuals: This is $\overline{Y}$ for freshmen; we obtain the $\overline{Y}$ for

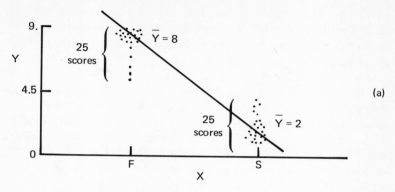

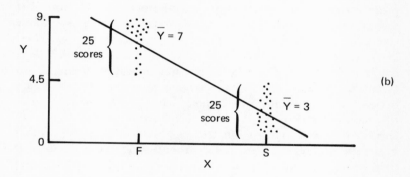

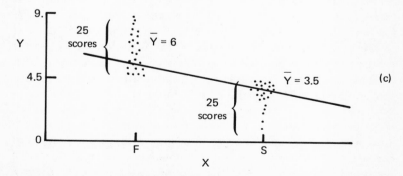

Figure 7-5. Some possible regressions from various perfect relationships.

seniors by adding *their* scores and dividing by 25, the number of senior individuals. We could do this for the other two sets of freshmen and seniors (Figures 7–4a and 7–4b) on the basis of the mean scores they obtained.

We see at once that the *slope* of the line we have drawn is not the same for all three sets of freshmen and seniors. It is steepest in Figure 7–4a and least steep in Figure 7–4c. Obviously, although the relationship is a perfect one, it is "more perfect" in case *a* than in case *c*. Thus, the strength of any relationship must take into account the *spread* within the data of each category, or the amount of *variation* and its distribution *within* the categories, as well as *between* them.

The line drawn in these figures is called the *regression* of the one variable on the other. If the data on both axes are in units of an *interval scale*, we can compute the best possible line that can be drawn through the scattered points. The regression line shows us how much of a variation in Y results from a variation in X. The steeper the slope of the line, the larger the *slope coefficient, B* or $\beta$. The relative amount of scatter of the points is, of course, a measure of the degree to which X and Y are correlated. A *correlation coefficient* may be calculated for this, the most frequently used being the *Pearson product moment correlation coefficient*, designated $r$. This coefficient, like other measures of association, can range from 0 to 1, where 1 is perfect correlation. Intermediate values of $r$, lying between 0 and 1, are not directly useful except when comparing sets of data for which several $r$'s have been obtained. If $r$ is squared, however, it shows the amount of variation in Y explained by X. For example, if $r = .9$, then .81 (that is, $.9^2$), or 81 percent of the variation in Y, is explained by X. If $r = .5$, then $r^2 = .25$, so that only 25 percent of the variation in Y is explained. This variation is the scatter we see in the figures, all of which represent departures from the best line of regression that can be drawn between the points. If all the points fell exactly on the line, $r$ would be equal to 1., no matter what the slope of the line. The greater the number of points not falling on the line, the lower the value of $r$.

As already mentioned, regression lines and product moment correlation coefficients may be calculated only if both X and Y are intervally scaled. In our own case of freshmen and seniors *vs.* alienation scores, both X and Y are *ordinal scales*, and we cannot compute $B$ or $r$. However, if X were the variable, *education*, operationalized into *years of schooling*, and Y were some other intervally scaled indicator, such as *income*, operationalized into *dollars per year*, a regression line could be computed and the Pearson product moment correlation coefficient obtained also. One sees these coefficients primarily in connection with survey research, but they have application in other areas as well.

Although correlation and regression coefficients appear to make maximal use of the available data obtained as a result of research efforts, their true utility in social research has been somewhat exaggerated. Aside from age, years, income, and some related demographic variables, very few concepts of sociological interest involve indicators that are true interval scales. Some sociologists, eager to apply sophisticated techniques, have attempted regression and correlation methods on noninterval scales. They treat ordinal scales *as if* they were interval scales. This, however, involves an intellectual compromise that not all methodologists are willing to commit. Just as a theory must be internally consistent, so must our methodology. Theory and method are the same thing. At the level of meaning, it makes little sense to pretend that we have a certain kind of scale when in fact we do not.

In student research, it may be useful to graph the results of one's study in terms of X and Y coordinates. The student research on *Time* magazine covers (Chapter 2) would have benefited from such a presentation. Since *number of covers* and *calendar year* are both intervally scaled, coefficients could have been computed. However, graphic presentation need not be limited to intervally scaled variables. In our Figures 7–4 through 7–5, we found it useful to indicate possible results on X and Y coordinates and gained increased insights, although our scale was only ordinal.

In this chapter we have been examining the manner in which concepts are associated. In attempting reductions of property space, what we seek to do is eliminate certain possible combinations that, however dictated, are not found in the empirical world, or are found in such small numbers as to make them of negligible importance in the matters we are considering. By so doing, we are attempting to clarify the association between concepts and, it is hoped, find fewer dimensions that characterize most of the cases under examination. In this sense a regression line also reduces property space: It indicates the best single dimension that can be found between the two concepts. The correlation coefficient measures the deviation of *all* the cases considered, even those found in small numbers, although they may contribute very little to the matters we are considering.

SUGGESTED READINGS

Blalock, Hubert, *Theory Construction* (Englewood Cliffs, N.J.: Prentice-Hall, 1972).

Kerlinger, Fred N., *Foundations of Behavioral Research* (New York: Holt, Rinehart & Winston, 1964).

Madge, John, *The Tools of Social Science* (New York: Anchor, 1965).

# 8

## *The House That Jack Built*

SOCIOLOGY, PARTICULARLY IN TIMES LIKE OUR OWN, is very much
like the house that Jack built in the nursery rhyme. "This is
the cat that ate the rat that ate the cheese . . ." It identifies one
concept after another and attempts to relate these concepts to
each other. *Description* and *identification* play major roles, and
the hope is that adequate description and careful identification
will enable us to detect some underlying structure holding together the world of social existence. If you remember the nursery
rhyme, you will recall that although we have descriptions of the
inhabitants of the house that Jack built, we are given no description of the house itself. This, too, is characteristic of sociology: It has not one but several architects, such as Max Weber,
Karl Marx, and Emile Durkheim, and innumerable master
carpenters, electricians, and bricklayers. Some of these "workers"
measure everything in sight, hoping for a good fit, although
there are no finished blueprints to tell them how to determine
what fit is good and what is not. Others mix metaphysical
mortar and dream of constructing a cathedral, patently ignoring
the rats or pretending that they do not exist. Most of them
ignore Jack, who lives in the house they are building. The very
last line of the nursery rhyme is simply, "And this is Jack."

The introduction to this book includes a quotation from Carl

Sandburg: "Man is a long time coming/Man will yet win." That is to say, Jack is a long time coming. He has been relegated to the very end of the nursery rhyme. But he will win out, with or without the help of sociologists. The problem is simply whether or not we, as sociologists, are interested in helping Man win. The first step we must take is to acknowledge that this is, after all, his house, not ours, that is being built.

But it *is* a house; it has *empirical* existence. Any social research must acknowledge its empirical nature. This presents several problems.

Sociologists, like Jack, live in a number of worlds. We have already discussed the middle-class bias of much of sociology, a bias that will, it is hoped, diminish now that we have brought it under scrutiny. There are other biases as well. One takes the form of antiempiricism. This bias is particularly strong in the work of philosophically oriented students and is traceable to the reaction against *positivism*. The philosophical doctrines generally lumped together as positivistic are so many and so varied that an accurate definition of positive philosophy is probably no longer possible. In the social sciences generally, *positivism* is associated with the name of August Comte (1798–1857), a French philosopher of the time of Napoleon who wrote a six-volume work entitled *Positive Philosophy*. Comte invented the word *sociology* (from the Latin word *socius*, associate, and the Greek word *logos*, word or reason). Thus, he envisioned sociology as the science of human association. He dreamed of a social physics, was committed to the notion of progress, and believed in the existence of social laws, similar if not identical to natural laws, which could be determined. Once this was done, everyone could live together in peace and harmony, and there would no longer be a need for such bloody debacles as the French Revolution. *Reason* would prevail. Comte's positive philosophy shared much of the optimistic view of the physical sciences espoused by Claude Henri de Saint-Simon (1760–1825).

Although traces of this philosophy are found in all the social sciences,* particularly psychology, sociologists today are far less certain than Comte was that any general social laws may be determined, or that reason will ultimately triumph in human

---

* The very fact that they consider themselves as *sciences* is sufficient proof of this.

affairs. Experience and reason are not such harmonious bed-fellows as some of the heirs of the French Revolution assumed. Our own century has provided abundant proof of this. All of Max Weber's idealistic sociological speculation, as well as his own role in helping to draft the Weimar Republic's constitution after World War I, could not avert the rise of Hitler Germany, which led to World War II. Indeed, we have witnessed more warfare and more bloodshed in our own time than in any other period of history, despite the widely proclaimed emergence of reason into human affairs and history. Although we still do not know very much about Jack, we do know that he is no angel, nor any similar embodiment of love. Perhaps, as Sandburg suggests, he has not as yet attained his inherent possibilities; perhaps he will always be "on the way" to arriving and never arrive, whether he wins or not. In short, Man is a great deal more complex than Saint-Simon, Comte, Weber, and Marx gave him credit for being. Our role, as sociologists, is to attempt to understand Jack (and Jill) rather than to determine universal laws about him. *Understanding* may be more important than *prediction*. Laws are useful primarily for prediction, or control. Thus the purposes of the social sciences must be viewed as differing from those of the natural sciences.

The confusion is compounded by the fact that the natural sciences deal with the empirical world. If the purposes of the natural and the social sciences differ, the argument runs, then perhaps the social sciences are not or should not be concerned with the empirical world. This is a curiously involuted kind of reasoning. If we, as social scientists, are not to concern ourselves with what does in fact occur, with the world as it is, then with what are we to concern ourselves? With the world as it *should* be? What it should be is the concern of philosophy and religion, not of science. Unless we are willing to reject the real world of people and activity and lose ourselves in wishful speculation and fantasies of what might be, there appears to be nothing else for us to do than engage in an attempt to understand people and activity as they exist, or have existed. This is empirical study.

If we are engaged in historical sociological research, this is none the less empirical, for it calls upon evidences of life as it has been lived by real people and leads us to make comparisons within and between categories, as in any other sociological analysis. Whether we are dealing with the microprocesses that take place within small groups of people or the macroprocesses of social development and organization, we need evidence to uphold arguments: Weber realized this, and so did Marx and Durkheim. Marx spent many years at the library of the British Museum, searching through innumerable volumes and calculating margins of profits, growth rates, and capital surpluses. Weber, too, was an economist. The notion that research can be nonempirical, or that anything mathematical was "nonsociological," would not have occurred to either of them, and had it been raised would have been immediately rejected. The great philosophers and social thinkers before them had all been trained as mathematicians. Indeed, the separation between mathematics and philosophy is purely arbitrary. Mathematics is a particular philosophical mode of expression: It is analysis at its highest level. The problem in sociology has not been related to the philosophical or analytical aspects of mathematics but to the abuse of its sound procedures by some sociologists in their applications of mathematics. Too often social scientists have employed mathematics, not out of respect for its analytical precision, but to give a spurious air of *scientism* to their work. And this approach has made mathematical methods suspect in many quarters. Mathematics and empiricism have unfortunately been lumped together in the minds of many students.

This is an unwarranted association. All social research is empirical research, although it is not all mathematical. All social research is analytical, although it is not all mathematical. In this volume we have seen some of the varieties of social research. At this point the student must have realized that whether a method is quantitative or qualitative, the procedures are the same. We are interested in the world of social activity at the level of conceptualization. Various research tools are available to us in our efforts to learn how society is possible. All we can do is arrange our concepts, whether we derive them before the fact or after the fact, in some ordering that helps us to understand what goes on about us. We should not hide behind either mathematics or philosophy in this attempt but should employ both sparingly, and only to make the kinds of distinctions necessary for purposes of analysis.

At this point in our history, we do not know how the world of social reality is constructed. Our first task is to find out what goes on in that world. This means that our sociology will be more descriptive and less theoretical than many earlier sociologists would have liked it to be. No one today can speak for sociology as a whole; sociology today is not what Comte dreamed of, and it probably never will be. There are many differing approaches to the study of society, and we must employ all of them if we are ever to penetrate the layers upon layers of meanings and actions that bind individuals together.

There is a world of numbers, and a number of worlds. The world of numbers has much to offer if one understands thoroughly what one is doing and can apply the proper methodology at the proper time to the proper area. But this holds true for the nonnumerical worlds as well; an absence of numbers does not make these worlds more "real," and may only make them more "false." The reason that a Marx and a Weber could perform the kinds of social analysis they did is related to the fact that both were mathematicians and therefore could isolate concepts, make comparisons between them and within them, and then order them sequentially so that they made the most sense. With the demise of classical education, which included drilling in highly systematized fields of learning, such as Latin and Greek, mathematics, history, and philosophy, most of us have been deprived of analytical methodology in its more creative aspects. We are thus forced to accept the social construction of reality forced upon us by our peer group: We live in the fads and fashions of our time. We are slaves to the ideas of our class, our generation, our nation, our friends and families. Karl Mannheim (1893–1947) was able to see through this and develop a sociology of knowledge that examines the wholly relativistic nature of thought and its products. For Mannheim, thought is predicated upon social existence. Hence it is that existence, with its divisions into social class and dominant ideologies, that must be studied. For Mannheim, it is the number of coexisting worlds that must be the focus of sociological study, not the world of numbers.

Other methodologists are more quantitatively inclined. Confronted with an infinity of possibilities, they select some few dozen and attempt to measure the degree of correlation between them, trying to determine the most likely *path* existing between them. *Path analysis* is a technique that selects many variables and attempts to show the contribution of each to the other. It uses expanded forms of Figure 6–1 (p. 136) and relates the variables to each other by path equations similar to the ones discussed in Chapter 7 under *regression*. By this procedure it shows which variables have the least effect in explaining the variation found in a related variable and which have the most effect. The variables must be intervally scaled and have the same kind of statistical distribution.

*Factor analysis* is another procedure for relating many variables to each other. Here *correlation coefficients* (Chapter 7) are computed between each variable and every other and the coefficients are placed in a *matrix* of rows and columns. By employing *matrix algebra*, a set of factors is obtained. Some variables *load* more heavily upon these factors than others, and the task is then one of identifying the factors *at the level of meaning* by examining the variables that give rise to them.

*Structural-effects analysis* seeks to determine whether some property of the individual increases or decreases as a function of his membership in a group. These are only a few of the more advanced techniques currently employed by those for whom the use of numbers does not represent a threat but a valuable research approach.

Good research, in order to be good, must continually subject itself to critical examination. Both mathematical and non-mathematical sociologists sometimes hide behind their methodology and lose sight of what it is they are seeking. A methodology is no substitute for theory, any more than a theory that ignores its methodological blunders is a substitute for common sense. In reading the results of any social research, certain fundamental questions must be kept in mind:

*Is it possible to obtain the kinds of data necessary to arrive at the results?* How might this be done? Can we rely upon this procedure to yield data that are not only true for the respondent but true in fact? If these are data derived from questioning individuals, can we be certain these are not simply normative responses—that is, that the respondents are not simply giving us the answers they presume we want them to give? If the data are based upon historical materials, can we be certain that they are not ideologically slanted to present the best side of the picture as seen by the author of the material?

If someone were to publish results claiming that this generation of young women menstruate at earlier ages than their grandmothers did, would you believe it? Because of our notions of social progress and the presumed "advancement" of women, we might be tempted to. But a moment's reflection tells us that, even if this were true, we would have no way of knowing it. While there may indeed be very good records on the present generation of women, the data on grandmothers are undoubtedly very scanty indeed. In those days women were not asked such questions. And in earlier times still?

*Is it possible to compare the concepts compared in this research?* Are the levels of abstraction the same or different? What is the unit of analysis? Does the researcher commit any logical fallacies in reaching conclusions based upon his data? Are the appropriate scales employed, or does the researcher hedge on the use of ordinal scales where the methodology demands interval scales? Does he divide scales that cannot be divided? Multiply them? Compare them on a percentage basis? If the research involves operationalization, how adequate are the operational definitions? Can you think of better ones?

*If a causal relationship is asserted, has it indeed been shown?* Or has only correlation been shown? Remember that correlation does not show causality, although the absence of correlation shows the absence of causality. Remember, too, that the dependent variable can change only *after* the application of an independent variable if causality is involved.

*What* a priori *assumptions have been made?* Have these all been acknowledged by the author, or is there some secret demon he is concealing from us? What are his biases?

If such questions are kept in mind when reading the research results of others, then our own research efforts will (or should) soon improve in quality. It is very easy, as Hamlet's girl friend knew, to be critical of the route trodden by others while we ourselves whizz down the primrose path, enjoying what we do and unmindful of the dangers to our fellows. If we are honest in our determination to discover something about the world we live in, we will learn from the mistakes of others and avoid the primrose path. We will learn as many research techniques as possible and then, after applying them discriminately, select those that give us the greatest yield in meaningful results. Then perhaps sociology will one day resemble something other than the house that Jack built. Precisely what it will resemble depends upon the honesty and strength of your convictions. Who knows? You may even discover the true identity of Jack.

SUGGESTED READINGS

Blau, Peter M., "Structural Effects," *American Sociological Review* 15 (August, 1960).

Blumer, Herbert, "What Is Wrong with Social Theory?" in William J. Filstead (ed.) *Qualitative Methodology* (Chicago: Markham, 1970).

Miley, James D., and Michael Micklin, "Structural Change and the Durkheimian Legacy," *American Journal of Sociology* 78 (November, 1972).

Runciman, W. G., *A Critique of Max Weber's Philosophy of Social Science* (Cambridge, England: Cambridge University Press, 1972).

Taylor, K. W., and James Frideres, "Issues Versus Controversies: Substantive and Statistical Significance," *American Sociological Review* 37 (August, 1972).

Von Mises, Richard, *Positivism: A Study in Human Understanding* (New York: Dover, 1968).

Wallace, Walter, *The Logic of Science in Sociology* (Chicago: Aldine Atherton, 1971).

Weber, Max, *The Methodology of the Social Sciences* (New York: Free Press, 1969).

Whitehead, Alfred North, *Science and the Modern World* (New York: Free Press, 1967).

# Index